PRAISE FOR

SCRIPTURE PUZZLERS

"*Scripture Puzzlers* will reinforce what the students have learned from the scripture mastery verses in seminary in a fun and challenging way."

—Terry Deighton, seminary instructor, Sedro-Woolley, WA

"These puzzles are presented in a fun and entertaining way [and help] future missionaries, seminary students, and teachers as they commence their journey toward scriptural mastery."

—Donna Fuller, author of *A Strand of Doubt*

"These puzzles are awesome! I wish my teachers had given us these when I was in seminary. They give opportunities not only to learn the doctrine of Christ but to have fun doing it!"

—Elder Ryan Corbett, Vancouver Washington Mission

"As an early morning seminary teacher, I believe these puzzles can be a benefit to the seminary classroom. The puzzles create a fun atmosphere in which to learn the required scriptures. By requiring outside-the-box thinking, the puzzles reinforce the scripture passages without boring rote memorization. It was enjoyable to watch the students work on them individually and in small groups."

—Melanie Kitchens, seminary instructor, Longview, WA

"These puzzles were a fun and helpful tool for my seminary students to learn and understand the scripture masteries."

—Leanne Jones, early morning seminary instructor, Longview, WA

"These [puzzles] are challenging and engaging! My young adult children and I love solving them during family home evening or for a spiritual Sunday activity. They are such a useful resource in our home because they are both entertaining and educational. We're becoming real master scriptorians!"

—Shelly Ditzler, home-schooling mom, Woodland, WA

SCRIPTURE PUZZLERS

[CROSSWORDS, WORD SEARCHES, AND OTHER BRAIN TEASERS]

MARYALICE WALLIS

AND

CHARLOTTE LINDSTROM

CFI
An imprint of Cedar Fort, Inc.
Springville, Utah

ISBN 13: 978-1-4621-1548-8

Published by CFI, an imprint of Cedar Fort, Inc.
2373 W. 700 S., Springville, UT 84663
Distributed by Cedar Fort, Inc., www.cedarfort.com

LIBRARY OF CONGRESS CONTROL NUMBER: 2014953058

Cover design by Shawnda T. Craig
Cover design © 2015 Lyle Mortimer
Edited and typeset by Jessica B. Ellingson
Authors' photographs taken by Krista M. Cooley and Amanda L. Wallis

Printed in the United States of America

10 9 8 7 6 5 4 3 2 1

Printed on acid-free paper

CONTENTS

HELLO PUZZLERS!

It has been our pleasure writing *Scripture Puzzlers* for your enjoyment. Our hope is that the spirit of this book will be felt as you gain a greater understanding of and begin to master the scriptures.

The puzzles in this book are all original and are crafted to enhance your study of the standard works, whether for personal study, missionary preparation, seminary education, or just plain fun. Each section of the book has a collection of twenty-five puzzles that are aimed at aiding in the memorization of scriptures based on the seminary scriptures for each volume of scripture. Additionally, there are ten puzzles for each volume of scripture that pertains to keywords or the application of the principles taught in the scripture. A "Tips for Solving" page is included to help you solve some of the more difficult puzzle types. Answer keys are found at the end of the book, and an index is included that contains hints and the reference for each puzzle's scripture.

May you find joy in searching the scriptures in an entertaining way!

All the best,
MaryAlice Wallis
Charlotte Lindstrom

TIPS FOR SOLVING

TIPS FOR SOLVING CODE PUZZLES

1. Start with one-letter words. There are only two: I and a.
2. E T A O I N. These are the most frequently used letters (in order of frequency).
3. Remember contractions and possessives. These will be easy to spot because they have an apostrophe. For example: *don't*, *doesn't*, *he's*, and *they're*. In the scriptures, contractions aren't used. For example, they will use *cannot* instead of *can't*.
4. Attack the two- and three-letter words. Look for common words (*on, in, am, and, the*). Don't forget scripture words like *ye*, *lo*, *yea*, and *woe*.
5. Look for digraphs. Some examples are -h (th, ch, sh, ph, wh), -k (ck, lk), qu, ex. Also look for double-letter digraphs: ee, ll, oo, dd, nn.
6. Consider prefixes and suffixes. Prefix examples: de-, dis-, mis-, pre-, re-. Suffix examples: -able, -er, -ness, -ment, -ous, -eth
7. Don't forget common scripture words, For example, *hath, hast, shall, thee, thou, thus, unto*.
8. Watch for telltale word patterns. Examples: a – – a – – (always), e – e – (ever or even), – e – e – (never), e – e – – (every), – e o – – e (people).
9. Consider the source. There are differences in the writing styles between each book of scripture and even between authors. Think of the difference in word choice and sentence structure between Isaiah, "And it shall come to pass in the last days, that the mountain of the Lord's house shall be established in the top of the mountains" (Isaiah 2:2), and Genesis, "And the Lord God called unto Adam, and said unto him, Where art thou?" (Genesis 3:9).
10. Trial and error. Don't discount this strategy, but remember that no letter will represent itself. Good luck!

TIPS FOR SOLVING LETTER DROP PUZZLES

1. Don't forget digraphs, prefixes and suffixes, common words, and telltale word patterns. See the details on these under "Tips for solving code puzzles."
2. Compare the columns that contain highlighted letters. Compare the letters between columns that have highlighted letters beneath them. The one letter that appears in each column would be the highlighted letter.
3. Check the columns with the fewest letters. These are usually the columns on the ends, and by process of elimination, you can determine which letter goes where.
4. Notice where letters are dropping. Is the letter dropping into the beginning, middle, or end of a word? It's not likely to be a vowel at the end of a word unless it's an E; occasionally it may be an O, as in *unto*.

OLD TESTAMENT PUZZLERS

BECOMING ONE

[WORD SEARCH]

Search forward, backward, up, down, and diagonally to find the words and phrases missing from the scripture below. If a word is repeated, it is marked with a symbol. Unscramble the intersecting letters to find the final theme. Check page 163 for the reference and a hint.

C	C	N	O	M	D	N	A	H	T	I	O	B	J	S	O	U	J
L	H	B	E	F	E	E	I	V	Y	P	N	N	H	L	P	I	U
J	O	I	N	G	K	N	P	B	U	A	E	M	G	W	M	Y	D
E	N	V	L	H	L	T	I	N	R	S	C	P	F	E	I	T	A
R	Y	C	R	D	W	Y	Z	H	S	D	N	H	H	R	A	R	H
T	U	X	T	G	R	U	X	S	T	O	A	R	I	R	H	R	S
Y	I	Z	Y	I	O	E	C	A	I	Y	N	T	L	N	A	W	P
U	O	O	D	J	A	T	N	J	C	U	O	O	U	E	N	I	O
I	P	K	U	R	S	I	O	H	K	P	T	T	F	I	S	K	M
H	X	J	I	C	O	R	P	F	D	I	H	Y	U	M	D	H	U
O	O	H	O	V	H	W	W	S	A	O	E	I	P	T	A	J	Y
S	C	U	P	B	G	B	N	M	E	R	R	J	C	E	W	N	T
P	V	I	S	R	A	E	L	U	I	P	O	S	O	D	F	V	R
C	B	G	M	E	C	O	M	P	A	N	I	O	N	S	N	B	E
D	N	D	R	N	K	R	U	K	L	Y	U	F	F	C	E	S	H
F	M	S	E	G	L	E	H	J	R	T	P	D	H	L	V	P	M
G	A	F	M	F	W	L	O	R	D	E	S	A	J	K	B	N	H

Theme: Two _ _ _ _ _ _ _ _ _ _ of Jesus Christ

The __________ of the __________ came again unto me, saying, Moreover, thou _____ ____ ______, take thee one ♥__________, and ♦________ upon it, For __________, and for the __________ of ♣__________ his ♠__________: then take ☼ __________ ♥__________, and ♦________ upon it, For __________, the ♥__________ of __________, and for all the __________ of ♣__________ his ♠__________: And __________ them ●______ to ☼__________ into ●______ ♥______; and they shall become ●______ in __________ _______ .

BELIEVE AND KNOW

[CROSSWORD]

Use the clues given inside the passage to find the answers to the crossword and complete the scripture. Some words may be repeated. Check page 163 for the reference and a hint.

Wherefore the [13↓ another name for the Savior] said, Forasmuch as this [12→ ♦inhabitants of the world] draw [1→ opposite of far] me with their [8↓ where food is chewed], and with their [13→ outline of the mouth] do honour me, but have [2↓ taken away] their [14→ pumps blood through the body] far from me, and their [5↓ to be afraid] toward me is [15↓ instructed] by the [7↓ something upon which another idea is built] of [9↓ counterpart of women]: Therefore, behold, I will [6→ continue] to do a [10→ ♠ tremendous; miraculous] [11→ ♥ labor] among this [12→ ♦], even a [10→ ♠] [11→ ♥] and a [11↓ a miracle; cause for amazement]: for the [4→ knowlegde] of their [3↓ those that brought gifts to baby Jesus—two words] shall perish, and the [16→ knowing; comprehending] of their [18→ wise; sensible] men shall be [17→ concealed].

CHERISHED GIFTS FROM GOD

[MATCHING]

Match the reference with the key words for each scripture. Write the letter from the right column on the line with the corresponding number to find the final theme for Psalm 127:3. Check pages 163–64 for a hint.

1. Moses 7:18	Ye shall be a holy nation. (I)
2. Abraham 3:22–23	Clean hands, and a pure heart. (A)
3. Genesis 2:24	A marvellous work and a wonder. (L)
4. Exodus 19:5–6	Abraham was chosen before he was born. (E)
5. Joshua 24:15	Elijah will turn the hearts of fathers and children. (G)
6. Psalms 24:3–4	The law of the fast. (O)
7. Malachi 4:5–6	Zion––one heart and one mind in righteousness. (H)
8. Isaiah 1:18	Jeremiah was foreordained before birth. (R)
9. Isaiah 29:13–14	Husbands and wives should be one. (R)
10. Isaiah 58:6–7	Choose to serve the Lord. (T)
11. Jeremiah 1:4–5	God reveals His secret to His prophets. (D)
12. Amos 3:7	Though your sins be as scarlet. (E)

Children are an __ __ __ __ __ __ __ __ of the __ __ __ __.
1 2 3 4 5 6 7 8   9 10 11 12

CHOSEN ONES

[WORD SCRAMBLE]

Unscramble the words listed below. Place the unscrambled words on the correct lines in the passage to reveal the scripture. If a word is repeated, it is marked with a symbol. Check page 164 for the reference and a hint.

yhol tnaoin	eboy
epeplo	evico
oswrd	kpesa
rteha	eaiplruc
ncotenav	erurtase
nogmkdi	spteris
eIalrs	ecihnldr

Now therefore, if ye will _ _ _ _ my _ _ _ _ _ indeed, and keep my _ _ _ _ _ _ _ _, then ye shall be a _ _ _ _ _ _ _ _ _ _ _ _ _ _ _ _ unto me above all _ _ _ _ _ _: for all the _ _ _ _ _ is mine: And ye shall be unto me a _ _ _ _ _ _ _ of _ _ _ _ _ _ _, and an _ _ _ _ _ _ _ _ _ _. These are the _ _ _ _ _ which thou shalt _ _ _ _ _ unto the _ _ _ _ _ _ _ _ of _ _ _ _ _ _.

CLAIM YOUR BLESSINGS!

[WORD SCRAMBLE]

Unscramble the words listed below. Place the unscrambled words on the correct lines in the passage to reveal the scripture. If a word is repeated, it is marked with a symbol. Check page 164 for the reference and a hint.

uerp	igomdkn
asoirdncen	tpenre
alcestile	otywrh
etenr	ltepme

If we __ __ __ __ __ __ and live __ __ __ __ lives, then we are __ __ __ __ __ __ to receive __ __ __ __ __ __ __ __ __ __ __ __ __ __ __ __ __ and __ __ __ __ __ the __ __ __ __ __ __ __ __ __ __ __ __ __ __ __ __.

CLEAN THROUGH HIM

[HIDDEN MESSAGE]

Starting at the marked word, follow the directions to choose the words on the table. Write the words in the spaces to reveal a scripture with a great blessing. Some words may be used more than once. Check page 164 for the reference.

your	red	they	now	shall	be
as	★Come	sins	wool	Lord	the
saith	us	let	crimson	together	scarlet
reason	snow	though	like	and	white

Begin ★ ___________

Right 2, up 1 ___________,

Down 3, right 1 ___________

Up 1, left 2 ___________

Left 1 ___________

Down 1, left 1 ___________

Up 1, right 4 ___________,

Left 4 ___________

Up 1, right 5 ___________

Left 1 ___________:

Down 1, left 2 ___________

Up 3, left 2 ___________

Down 1, right 2 ___________

Right 3, up 1 ___________

Left 5, down 1 ___________

Down 1, right 5 ___________,

Left 3, up 2___________

Right 2 ___________

Right 1 ___________

Down 1, left 5 ___________

Right 5, down 2 ___________

Left 5, up 2 ___________

Right 1, Down 2 ___________;

Right 1 ___________

Up 3 ___________

Right 3 ___________

Left 4 ___________

Down 3, right 2 ___________

Up 1 ___________,

Up 2, left 1 ___________

Right 2 ___________

Right 1 ___________

Down 1, left 5 ___________

Right 3 ___________.

COMING PROMISE

[WORD SCRAMBLE]

Unscramble the words listed below. Place the unscrambled words on the correct lines in the passage to reveal the scripture. If a word is repeated, it is marked with a symbol. Check page 164 for the reference and a hint.

nubder

gimnoc

yad

leepop

cieacsrif

oSn fo nMa

higntti

dihtet

yotda

Behold, now it is called _ _ _ _ _ until the ♪ _ _ _ _ _ _ of the _ _ _ _ _ _ _ _, and verily it is a ♥_ _ _ of _ _ _ _ _ _ _ _ _ _ _, and a ♥_ _ _ for the _ _ _ _ _ _ _ _ of my _ _ _ _ _ _ _; for he that is _ _ _ _ _ _ _ shall not be _ _ _ _ _ _ _ at his ♪ _ _ _ _ _ _. (Doctrine and Covenants 64:23)

COVENANT KEEPERS

[WORD SEARCH]

Search forward, backward, up, down, and diagonally to find the words and phrases missing from the scripture below. If a word is repeated, it is marked with a symbol. Check page 164 for the reference and a hint.

A	H	C	H	O	O	S	E	A	O	G	L
L	E	R	E	G	N	T	E	H	K	A	S
B	O	V	C	D	O	I	D	F	N	O	R
F	Q	R	I	B	M	D	I	D	T	H	E
C	L	J	D	L	E	L	S	P	S	S	H
I	D	F	L	O	O	D	R	L	U	M	T
E	M	E	A	I	F	C	E	O	Y	K	A
K	W	D	C	G	D	K	H	C	E	D	F
D	G	S	E	R	V	E	T	B	J	A	E
A	N	S	C	T	N	M	O	H	W	I	B

And if it seem __________ unto you to ♥ ______________ the ♠ ______________,

______________ you this day __________ ye will ♥ ______________; whether the

♪ ______________which your ______________ ♥ ______________d that were on the

__________ __________ of the ______________, or the ♪ ______________ of the

Amorites, in whose ________________ ye ______________: but as for me and my

______________, we will ♥ ______________ the ♠ ______________.

ESTABLISH MY WORDS

[LETTER DROP]

Discover the scripture that applies to Ezekiel 37:15–17 by dropping the letters at the top into the correct boxes directly below them. Read the scripture left to right. Some words have been done for you. The highlighted spaces all contain the same letter. Check page 164 for a hint.

Wherefore, the Lord God will proceed to bring forth . . .

H	~~A~~	~~A~~	A	~~D~~	A	A	B	D	B	C	~~F~~	E	E	H	D	E	B	E	~~A~~	D
S	~~A~~	E	~~D~~	E	~~I~~	H	D	~~H~~	E	E	~~F~~	G	G	H	D	H	H	I	~~F~~	K
T	E	E	E	M	O	~~N~~	E	J	H	E	H	M	~~H~~		E	T	H	I	L	L
	E	H	M	S	T	N	O	L	~~I~~	I	T	N	N	~~I~~	O		S	~~O~~	M	~~S~~
	H	~~N~~	~~N~~	T	T	O	R	S	I	~~M~~	T	U	O	O	~~S~~		W	O	O	
	T	~~S~~		W	W	R	Y	T	W	~~O~~			O	O	S		W	O	R	
						R				~~O~~			T	S	T					
						W				S			T	T						
														U						
		░	■						■	O	F	■			░	■				;
■	A	N	D	■	I	N	■			░	■						■	O	F	■
■	A	S	■					■					░			░		■	A	S
	░	░		░			■	H	I	M	■					■				
	░	■	░									■	H	I	S	■				;
■	■	A	N	D	■			■		░	■					■				■
■					■		░		░			░			■			░	■	■
■	■	■	■	■					■	O	F	■			!	■	■	■	■	■

2 Nephi 27:14

FEEL HIS PRESENCE NEAR

[MATCHING]

Match the words in the left column with the words in the right column to complete each phrase of the scripture. Write the letter from the right column on the line with the corresponding number to find the final theme. Check page 164 for the reference.

1. Is not this the	burdens, (E)
2. to loose the	every yoke? (S)
3. to undo the heavy	that are cast out of thy house? (N)
4. and to let the oppressed	fast that I have chosen? (B)
5. and that ye break	to the hungry, (I)
6. Is it not to deal thy bread	bands of wickedness, (L)
7. and that thou bring the poor	from thine own flesh? (S)
8. when thou seest the naked,	go free, (S)
9. and that thou hide not thyself	that thou cover him; (G)

__ __ __ __ __ __ __ __ __
1 2 3 4 5 6 7 8 9

FLEE TEMPTATION

[LETTER DROP]

Discover the following scripture by dropping the letters at the top into the correct boxes directly below them. Read the scripture left to right. Some words have been done for you. The highlighted spaces all contain the same letter. Check page 165 for the reference and a hint.

There is none greater . . .

G ~~I~~ T	B H M ~~N~~ N R	A E E E O T	A C H I S T U	~~B~~ E H I K T T	A H I N N ~~U~~	A E R S ~~T~~ W	A ~~C~~ I N R T	~~A~~ C G H T Y	A H H H K ~~N~~ O	A E E I I T U	D E H I N S S T	E H I N S	B ~~D~~ E N T W	E G H I ~~O~~ S T	C E F G H S	A A E F O T	~~A~~ D H K N R U	E H I ~~N~~ O S	~~D~~ E I M O P S	T W
I	N	■		▒			■	▒					■		▒			■	;	■
■					▒			■	▒			▒	■	▒		■				
■					■				■		▒				■					■
■			■	B	U	T	■		▒		,	■								■
	▒			■				■	▒			■				:	■	▒		
■	■		▒			■	C	A	N	■		■	D	O	■		▒			■
					■										,	■	A	N	D	■
■	■	■				■								■			?	■	■	■

GUIDING BEACON

[SCRIPTURE FIND]

Find the missing words of each scripture. Write the found word from each scripture above the corresponding number in the final passage to reveal the theme. Check page 165 for the reference.

1. But (1)_____ (2) _______ must be fulfilled. Help thy servants to say, with thy grace assisting them: Thy will be done, O Lord, and not ours. (D&C 109:44)
2. For the commandment is (3)___ (4)_________; and the law is light; and reproofs of instruction are the way of life. (Proverbs 6:23)
3. The Lord God is my strength, and he will make (5)____ (6)______ like hinds' feet, and he will make me to walk upon mine high places. (Habakkuk 3:19)
4. Neither do men light a candle, and put it under a bushel, but on a candlestick; and it giveth (7)________ (8)_______ all that are in the house. (Matthew 5:15)
5. When my spirit was overwhelmed within me, then thou knewest (9)___ (10)______. In the way wherein I walked have they privily laid a snare for me. (Psalm 142:3)

_____ ______ is ___ _______ unto ___ ______, and a ________ _______ ___ _______.
1 2 3 4 5 6 7 8 9 10

HONOR THIS DAY

[MISSING-LETTER WORDS]

Every other letter is missing from the words in this scripture. The letters are listed in alphabetical order below. If a word is repeated, it is marked with a symbol. Check page 165 for the reference and a hint.

If thou __u__n __w__y ☼ __h__ f__o__ from the ♥ __a__b__t__, from ♪ __o__n__ ☼t__y ♦__l__a__u__e __n __y Ω__o__y __a__; and call the ♥ __a__b__t__ a ●__e__i__h__, the Ω__o__y __f __h__ Lord, __o__o__r__b__e; and shalt __o__o__r __i__, not ♪ __o__n__ ▲t__i__e ♣ __w__ w__y__, nor __i__d__n__ ▲t__i__e ♣__w__ ♦p__e__s__r__, nor __p__a__i__g ▲__h__n__ ♣o__n __o__d__: T__e__ s__a__t __h__u ●__e__i__h__ t__y__e__f in the Lord; and I __i__l __a__s__ ♠t__e__ t__ r__d__ u__o__ the __i__h __l__c__s of the __a__t__, and __e__d ♠__h__e __i__h the __e__i__a__e of Jacob ☼__h__ f__t__e__: for the mouth of the Lord hath spoken it.

a a a a a a a a a b b c d d d d d e e e e e e e e e e e f f g

g g g g g g h h h h h h h h h h h h h h h h h h i i i i i k l l

l l l l l l l m m n n n n n n n n n n o o o o o o o o p p p t t t

t t t t t t t t t r r r r r r s s s s s s s u u u u w w w w y y y

I WILL, I WILL

[HIDDEN MESSAGE]

Follow the code to find the corresponding words. Write the words on the spaces to discover a scripture with a great blessing. Some words may be used more than once. Fill in the words at the bottom of the puzzle to find the principle of the scripture. Check page 165 for the reference.

	1	2	3	4	5	6	7
A	in	vanity	sworn	shall	and	hath	or
B	into	Who	lifted	not	his	celestial	clean
C	a	temple	Lord	stand	that	nor	the
D	soul	pure	up	place	deceitfully	of	kingdom
E	hill	hands	holy	He	ascend	heart	unto

B2 ____________
A4 ____________
E5 ____________
B1 ____________
C7 ____________
E1 ____________
D6 ____________
C7 ____________
C3 ____________?
A7 ____________

B2 ____________
A4 ____________
C4 ____________
A1 ____________
B5 ____________
E3 ____________
D4 ____________?
E4 ____________
C5 ____________
A6 ____________

B7 ____________
E2 ____________,
A5 ____________
C1 ____________
D2 ____________
E6 ____________;
B2 ____________
A6 ____________
B4 ____________
B3 ____________

D3 ____________
B5 ____________
D1 ____________
E7 ____________
A2 ____________,
C6 ____________
A3 ____________
D5 ____________.

If we repent and live pure lives, then we are worthy to receive ____________ ordinances and enter the ____________ ____________.

LOOK INSIDE

[CROSSWORD]

Use the clues given to find answers to the crossword. Place the answers on the corresponding spaces in the scripture. Some words may be repeated. Check page 165 for the reference and a hint.

Across
2. To see
6. Opposite of inward
7. How tall you are
8. The way something looks
10. Looketh

Down
1. Seeth
2. Title of Jesus Christ
3. Face, visage
4. Height when upright
5. An adult male
7. Where you feel your emotions
9. Decline to do something

But the [2↓] ______ said unto Samuel, [2→] ________ not on his [3↓]______________, or on the [7→] ___________ of his [4↓] _________; because I have [9↓] ___________ him: for the [2↓] ________ [10→] ___________ not as [5↓] ________ [10→] ___________; for [5↓] _______ [1↓] ___________ on the [6→] _________ [8→] _______________, but the [2↓] _______ [1↓] ___________ on the [7↓] _________.

MAN OF GRIEF

[LETTER CLUE]

Fill in the answer to each clue. Write the numbered letters from the answers above the corresponding numbers in the final scripture. If a word is repeated, it is marked with a symbol. Check page 165 for the reference and a hint.

1. Redeemer 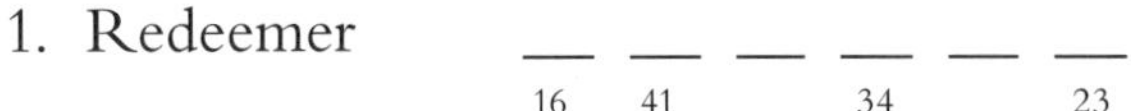
   ___ ___ ___ ___ ___ ___
   16 41 34 23

2. Ransom of mankind ___ ___ ___ ___ ___ ___ ___ ___ ___
   53 8 4 40 27 11

3. The act of being raised from the dead ___ ___ ___ ___ ___ ___ ___ ___ ___ ___ ___ ___
   14 55 26 46 49 42 36 30

4. The Savior of mankind ___ ___ ___ ___ ___ ___ ___ ___ ___ ___ ___
   43 12 50 51 29 38

5. Separation from God ___ ___ ___ ___ ___ ___ ___ ___ ___ ___ ___ ___ ___ ___
   17 39 31 3 5 52 45

6. Enduring pain or distress ___ ___ ___ ___ ___ ___ ___ ___ ___ ___
   44 33 37 47 20 13

7. Having the necessary ability to do something ___ ___ ___ ___ ___ ___ ___ ___ ___
   32 24 10 54 18 28

8. The power by which the earth was created ___ ___ ___ ___ ___ ___ ___ ___ ___ ___
   9 25 6 21 35 56

9. Flesh and bone ___ ___ ___ ___
   22 2 7

10. The ability to use the priesthood ___ ___ ___ ___ ___
    48 19 1 15

But he was ___ ___ ___ ___ ___ ___ ___ (1 2 3 4 5 6 7) for our ___ ___ ___ ___ ___ ___ ___ ___ ___ ___ ___ ___ ___ ___ (8 9 10 11 12 13 14 15 16 17 18 19 20 21), he was ___ ___ ___ ___ ___ ___ ___ (22 23 24 25 26 27 28) for our ___ ___ ___ ___ ___ ___ ___ ___ ___ ___ (29 30 31 32 33 34 35 36 37 38): the chastisement of our ___ ___ ___ ___ ___ (39 40 41 42 43) was upon him; and with his ___ ___ ___ ___ ___ ___ ___ (44 45 46 47 48 49 50) we are ___ ___ ___ ___ ___ ___ (51 52 53 54 55 56).

MY GLORY

[CODE]

Each letter in the passage has been changed to a different letter. For example, N has been changed to F (f = n). Crack the code to find the scripture principle. Check page 165 for the reference and a hint.

Wju exrjzl, crty ty od vjus qfl od azjud—cj eutfa cj bqyy crx toojucqztcd qfl xcxufqz ztwx jw oqf.

NEVER LED ASTRAY

[CODE]

Each letter in the passage has been changed to a different letter. For example, O has been changed to Q (Q = O). Crack the code to find the scripture principle. Check page 166 for the reference and a hint.

JKBMAN HPM AQGF BQF LOAA FQ CQHPOCB, RKH PM GMXMEAMHP POJ JMTGMH KCHQ POJ JMGXECHJ HPM DGQDPMHJ.

NO MATTER WHAT

[MATCHING]

Match the reference with the key words for each scripture. Write the letter from the right column on the line with the corresponding number to find the final theme. Check page 166 for the reference and a hint.

1. Genesis 39:9	The Ten Commandments. (R)
2. Moses 1:39	God's word is a lamp unto my feet. (L)
3. Isaiah 58:13–14	God created man in His own image. (S)
4. Genesis 1:26–27	Jesus Christ bore our griefs and suffered for our sins. (O)
5. Malachi 3:8–10	The Lord looks on the heart. (I)
6. 1 Samuel 16:7	Woe unto them that call evil good. (D)
7. Ezekiel 37:15–17	This is God's work and glory. (R)
8. Psalm 119:105	Joseph resisted temptation. (T)
9. Isaiah 53:3–5	Paying tithing brings blessings. (T)
10. Exodus 20:3–17	The Sabbath is the Lord's holy day. (U)
11. Isaiah 5:20	The Bible and the Book of Mormon are joined together. (N)

_ _ _ _ _   _ _ the _ _ _ _.
1 2 3 4 5   6 7   8 9 10 11

OFFERINGS AND BLESSINGS

[SCRIPTURE FIND]

Choose the correct bolded word or phrase for the following scriptures. Write the chosen word from each scripture above the corresponding number in the final passage to reveal the theme. Check page 166 for the reference and a hint.

1. Now therefore ye are [**cursed** or **bound**], and there shall none of you be freed from being bondmen, and hewers of wood and drawers of water for the [**temple** or **house**] of my God. (Joshua 9:23)

2. And they began to be a very industrious people; yea, and they were friendly with the Nephites; therefore, they did [**begin** or **open**] a correspondence with them, and the [**condemnation** or **curse**] of God did no more follow them. (Alma 23:18)

3. And again, they were wroth with him because he departed into the wilderness as the Lord had commanded him, and took the records which were engraven on the plates of brass, for they said that he [**stole from** or **robbed**] them. (Mosiah 10:16)

4. Nor consider that it is expedient for us, that one man should die for the people, and that the [**whole nation** or **entire country**] perish not. (John 11:50)

5. Thus saith the [**Lord of hosts** or **Lord of the whole earth**], the God of Israel; As yet they shall use this speech in the land of Judah and in the cities thereof, when I shall [**cause** or **bring**] again their captivity; The Lord bless thee, O habitation of justice, and mountain of holiness. (Jeremiah 31:23)

6. And verily they that are of the sons of Levi, who [**obtain** or **receive**] the office of the priesthood, have a commandment to take [**tithes** or **donations**] of the people according to the law, that is, of their brethren, though they come out of the loins of Abraham. (Hebrews 7:5)

7. And again, let the bishop appoint a [**steward** or **storehouse**] unto this church; and let all things both in money and in [**meat** or **food**], which are more than is needful for the wants of this people, be kept in the hands of the bishop. (D&C 51:13)

8. Examine me, O Lord, and [**try me** or **prove me**]; try my reins and my heart. (Psalm 26:2)

9. Pray always, and I will [**flow** or **pour**] out my Spirit upon you, and great shall be your [**blessing** or **gift**]—yea, even more than if you should obtain treasures of earth and corruptibleness to the extent thereof. (D&C 19:38)

10. Is there not [**sufficient space** or **room enough**] on the mountains of Adam-ondi-Ahman, and on the plains of Olaha Shinehah, or the land where Adam dwelt, that you should covet that which is but the drop, and neglect the more weighty matters? (D&C 117:8)

11. In the six hundredth year of Noah's life, in the second month, the seventeenth day of the month, the same day were all the fountains of the great deep broken up, and the [**gates** or **windows**] of [**heaven** or **paradise**] were opened. (Genesis 7:11)

Ye are (1) ____________ with a (2) _________: for ye have (3) __________ me, even this (4) ___________ __________. (5) ________ ye all the (6)_______ into the (7) __________________, that there may be (7) _______ in mine (1)__________, and (8)________ ___ now herewith, saith the (5) ______ (5) ___ (5) ________, if I will not (2) ______ you the (11) _________ of (11) __________, and (9) _______ you out a (9) ____________, that there shall not be (10) ______ ___________ to (6) __________ it.

ON THE SIXTH DAY

[CROSSWORD]

Use the clues given to find answers to the crossword. Place the answers on the corresponding spaces in the scripture. Some words may be repeated. Check page 166 for the reference and a hint.

Across
1. Moving slowly
3. Cows or steers
6. A person, man
8. What we breathe
9. The power to rule over
12. Body of salt water
13. A person, woman
14. A species that lives in water

Down
1. Formed or made
2. Our planet
4. To create, cause to happen
5. Woman's counterpart
7. Semblance; similar in appearance
10. Opposite of under
11. A reproduction or imitation of a person or thing
14. A bird of any kind

And God said, Let us [4↓] _______ [5↓] _______ in our [11↓] _________, after our [7↓] ____________: and let them have [9→] ____________________ [10↓] ________ the [14→] _________ of the [12→] ________, and [10↓] ________ the [14↓] ________ of the [8→] ____, and [10↓] _______ the [3→] _________, and [10↓] ______ all the [2↓] ________, and [10↓] _______ every [1→] _____________ thing that creepeth upon the [2↓] ________.

So God [1↓] ___________ [5↓] ______ in his own [11↓] _________, in the [11↓] ________ of God [1↓] ____________ he him; [6→] _______ and [13→] ________ [1↓] ___________ he them.

OLD TESTAMENT PUZZLERS

SCRIPTURE PUZZLERS

PRECIOUS ONES

[CODE]

Each word in the passage has been changed to numbers. Solve the mathematical equations to match the words with the numbers. Some words may be used more than once. Check page 166 for the reference and a hint.

15, 12 6 20 18 9 10 25: 14 10 30 9 10 28 27 24 45.

5 + 1	are
2 x 5	the
3 x 4	children
7 + 7	and
7 x 4	womb
9 + 9	heritage
3 x 8	his
3 x 5	Lo
6 x 5	fruit
5 x 5	Lord
3 x 9	is
4 x 5	an
9 x 5	reward
3 x 3	of

PREMORTAL BEINGS

[HIDDEN MESSAGE]

Solve the word puzzles in the passage below to complete the scripture. Some words may be repeated. Check page 167 for the reference and a hint.

Now the Lord had shown unto me, (cab – c + graham – g), the (pint – p + jelly – j – y + pig – p + fences – f) that were (pork – p – k + gain – i + prized – pr) before the (sword – s – d + cold – co) was; and (ham – h + song – s) all these there were many of the (knob - k + mile - mi) and (grape - ape + heat - h) ones; And God saw these (soon - on + mules – m – e) that they were (gum - um + food - f), and he stood in the (timid - ti + star – ar) of them, and he said: These I will make my (run – n + pliers – p – i); for he stood among those that were (wasp – wa + fire – f – e + splits – spl), and he saw that they were (gum – um + food - f); and he said unto me: (cab - c + graham - g), thou art one of them; thou wast (peach – pea + hose - h + man – ma) before thou wast (hobo - ho + barn – ba).

PRIESTHOOD KEYS RESTORED

[HIDDEN MESSAGE]

Solve the word puzzles in the passage below to complete the scripture. Some words may be repeated. Check page 167 for the reference and a hint.

(Able – a – l + hot – t + cold – co), I will send you (camelion – cam – on + jam – m + h) the (opposite of con + phone – on + t) before the (opposite of going) of the (grape – ap + cat – c) and (drain – ain + bread – br + fulfill – fill) day of the Lord: And he shall (tunnel – nnel + burn – bu) the (the – t + start – st) of the (faith – i + waters – wat) to the (chive – ve + cold – co + friend – f – i – d), and the (the – t + start – st) of the (chive – ve + cold - co + friend – f – i – d) to their (faith – i + waters – wat), lest I come and (plasma – pla – a + ignite – ign) the (bear – b + path – pa) with a (cat – at + purse – p).

PURIFIED BY OBEDIENCE

[CROSSWORD]

Use the clues below to determine the words that apply to the scripture found in Exodus 19:5–6. Answers are in order from top to bottom. The highlighted area gives the final theme. Check page 167 for a hint.

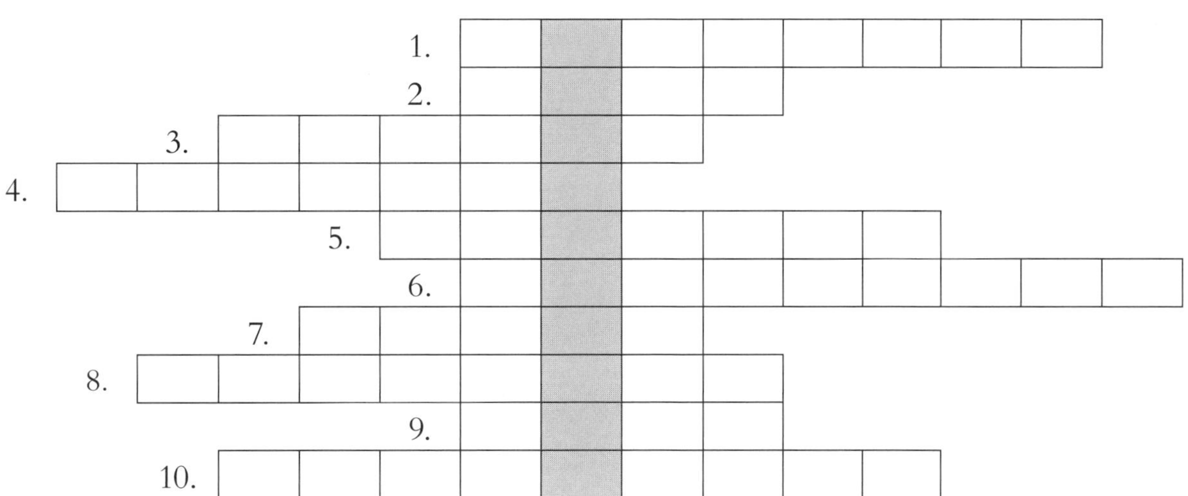

1. Offspring of parents
2. "Having a perfect brightness of ______." (2 Nephi 31:20)
3. Mother, father, and children
4. The pure love of Christ
5. The territory of Heavenly Father
6. Willingly giving up something important to you
7. Things hoped for but not seen
8. "For thou art an holy people unto the Lord thy God, and the Lord hath chosen thee to be a ____________ people unto himself." (Deuteronomy 14:2)
9. The greatest commandment
10. Oaths made with our Heavenly Father

RELY ON HIS GUIDANCE

[LETTER CLUE]

Fill in the answer to each clue. Write the numbered letters from the answers above the corresponding numbers in the final scripture. If a word is repeated, it is marked with a symbol. Check page 167 for the reference and a hint.

1. Applied knowledge ___ ___ ___ ___ ___ ___
   54 12 4 60 7
2. Gratefulness ___ ___ ___ ___ ___ ___ ___ ___ ___ ___ ___ ___
   1 15 46 27 51 32 6 13 37
3. To accept something as true, to trust ___ ___ ___ ___ ___ ___ ___
   16 20 61 56 28
4. The act of depending on ___ ___ ___ ___ ___ ___ ___ ___
   18 35 55 26 67 43 64 21
5. Education information ___ ___ ___ ___ ___ ___ ___ ___ ___
   33 30 63 41 58 14
6. Communication with God ___ ___ ___ ___ ___ ___
   66 2 49 47 8
7. The real facts about something ___ ___ ___ ___ ___
   24 36 3 5 69
8. Good and deserving respect ___ ___ ___ ___ ___ ___
   45 29 62 38 11
9. Serious difficulty, trials ___ ___ ___ ___ ___ ___ ___ ___ ___
   39 9 70 42 19
10. God's laws ___ ___ ___ ___ ___ ___ ___ ___ ___ ___ ___ ___
    50 17 31 34 40 65 48
11. Imparting knowledge ___ ___ ___ ___ ___ ___ ___ ___
    10 59 22 25 23 44
12. Following rules or laws ___ ___ ___ ___ ___ ___ ___ ___
    53 57 52 68

___ ___ ___ ___ ___ in the ___ ___ ___ ___ with all ♥ ___ ___ ___ ___ ___ ___ ___ ___ ___ ___; and
1 2 3 4 5 6 7 8 9 10 11 12 13 14 15 16 17 18 19

___ ___ ___ ___ not unto ♥ ___.
20 21 22 23 24 25 26 27 28 29 30 31 32 33 34 35 36 37 38 39 40 41 42 43 44

In all thy ___ ___ ___ ___ ___ ___ ___ ___ ___ ___ ___ ___ ___ ___ ___ him, and he shall
45 46 47 48 49 50 51 52 53 54 55 56 57 58 59

___ ___ ___ ___ ___ ___ thy ___ ___ ___ ___ ___.
60 61 62 63 64 65 66 67 68 69 70

THE LORD'S ERRAND

[CODE]

Each letter in the passage has been changed to a mathematical equation. For example, R = 30. Solve the equations to match the letters with the numbers. Check page 167 for the reference and a hint.

2 x 5   5 x 5   7 x 4   7 x 4   8 x 4   4 x 5

11 x 3   7 x 4

8 x 4   4 x 5   5 x 6   7 x 5   4 x 5

11 x 3   5 x 5   4 x 5

11 x 2   7 x 4   5 x 6   3 x 5

THE TEN COMMANDMENTS: PART 1

[WORD SEARCH]

Search forward, backward, up, down, and diagonally to find the words and phrases missing from the scripture below. If a word is repeated, it is marked with a symbol. Unscramble the intersecting letters to find the final theme. Check page 168 for the reference and a hint.

A	D	G	J	L	S	F	H	K	S	U	O	L	A	E	J	T	Y
E	C	H	I	L	D	R	E	N	P	O	Q	V	Z	D	F	H	B
L	S	D	E	P	O	I	G	O	D	X	C	V	A	J	L	E	N
C	O	F	C	A	X	U	H	B	N	M	M	S	D	I	N	M	W
I	G	R	T	Q	V	C	J	F	L	G	K	E	K	V	N	A	H
N	H	J	D	S	D	E	O	H	Q	W	G	Q	L	S	T	N	Z
I	K	L	Y	F	J	B	N	M	E	A	M	W	X	E	Q	C	X
Q	W	E	U	M	H	J	L	R	M	G	N	E	R	B	W	V	W
U	R	Y	E	E	R	N	K	I	F	A	B	R	C	G	O	D	S
I	T	R	I	T	W	Y	N	T	K	H	N	T	V	V	E	M	E
T	C	L	P	O	U	E	L	Y	D	E	V	D	B	C	R	N	R
Y	H	K	D	I	V	P	R	E	S	J	N	Y	M	X	H	E	T
V	B	W	S	A	I	U	V	U	P	K	C	E	N	E	Y	A	Y
N	O	V	R	X	L	O	H	I	O	L	X	O	S	M	N	R	U
B	C	G	U	I	L	T	L	E	S	S	T	Y	U	S	S	T	I
M	T	Y	A	U	I	S	Y	D	F	E	V	R	E	S	K	H	S
S	R	E	H	T	A	F	D	G	J	L	H	S	F	A	J	K	L

1. Thou shalt have no other ______ before me.

2. Thou shalt not make unto thee any ________ ________, or any __________ of any thing that is in __________ above, or that is in the ♥________ beneath, or that is in the ________ under the ♥________: Thou shalt not ______ ________ thyself to them, nor __________ them: for I the ●________ thy ☼________ am a __________ ☼______, visiting the __________ of the __________ upon the __________ unto the third and fourth generation of them that hate me; And shewing ________ unto thousands of them that ______ me, and keep my ______________.

3. Thou shalt not take the ________ of the ●______ thy ☼_____ in ♦______; for the ●______ will not hold him __________ that taketh his name in ♦______.

I am God _ _ _ _ _ _ _ _ _

THE TEN COMMANDMENTS: PART 2

[WORD SEARCH]

Search forward, backward, up, down, and diagonally to find the words and phrases missing from the scripture below. If a word is repeated, it is marked with a symbol. Unscramble the intersecting letters to find the final theme. Check page 168 for the reference and a hint.

C	V	S	B	P	N	U	V	R	L	S	B	A	W	M	I	O	G
O	K	T	N	A	V	R	E	S	D	I	A	M	O	L	O	R	D
I	G	H	K	V	D	D	L	L	W	F	E	R	T	Y	O	U	K
B	S	T	R	A	N	G	E	R	T	D	I	O	P	A	F	O	D
N	H	E	R	T	Y	U	I	W	R	T	A	R	F	G	B	B	C
M	D	O	Z	C	S	Q	W	E	O	G	A	U	E	L	V	A	F
W	F	E	L	V	B	A	T	Y	U	L	H	C	G	S	S	L	N
Q	G	S	R	Y	T	N	B	G	O	D	L	U	I	H	T	T	B
E	H	D	E	J	E	K	L	B	Y	T	U	A	A	S	T	E	M
R	J	F	G	V	W	E	R	S	A	P	O	S	H	D	F	E	D
T	K	S	A	H	E	G	O	L	F	T	D	A	O	G	H	X	R
Y	L	E	K	L	L	N	P	O	I	A	H	F	T	W	K	L	A
U	H	A	W	E	R	T	T	C	V	B	H	H	P	K	O	B	V
I	U	I	O	P	A	S	D	H	T	Y	T	H	Q	L	P	R	B
O	L	S	Z	D	A	U	G	H	T	E	R	T	E	O	M	N	K
P	I	K	N	I	P	R	I	A	N	T	A	I	O	R	C	V	B
X	O	P	A	S	D	F	M	A	N	S	E	R	V	A	N	T	U

4. Remember the ♠_________ day, to keep it _____. ♪____ days shalt thou _______, and do all thy ♥ ______: But the ☻___________ day is the ♠_________of the ♦_____ thy _____: in it thou shalt not do any ♥ ______, thou, nor thy ____, nor thy __________ , thy _____________ , nor thy ______________ , nor thy _________ , nor thy ___________ that is within thy gates: For in ♪____ days the ♦_____ made _________and ______, the ______ , and all that in them is, and __________ the ☻___________ day: wherefore the ♦_____ blessed the ♠_________day, and _____________ it.

Answer: _ _ _ _ _ _ _ _ _ _

THE TEN COMMANDMENTS: PART 3

[WORD SEARCH]

Search forward, backward, up, down, and diagonally to find the words and phrases missing from the scripture below. If a word is repeated, it is marked with a symbol. Unscramble the intersecting letters to find the final theme. Check page 168 for the reference and a hint.

B	P	A	G	A	I	N	S	T	L	P	O	I	L	R	E	T	Y
H	J	K	L	M	N	B	V	C	A	S	D	F	O	L	O	R	D
M	F	R	D	E	M	A	N	S	E	R	V	A	N	T	W	R	C
F	H	A	G	K	L	X	C	V	B	N	Y	M	G	G	R	T	R
G	Y	H	L	J	K	L	A	N	S	R	U	I	Y	P	T	A	A
S	C	X	V	S	F	J	K	L	E	O	P	W	D	S	D	F	E
B	N	M	Y	S	E	R	E	T	U	I	D	O	R	N	G	H	B
F	A	T	H	E	R	W	L	J	K	L	G	T	Y	U	A	T	Y
Z	S	C	V	B	N	U	I	Q	W	E	L	H	I	O	X	L	Z
N	P	T	X	P	D	M	J	T	T	Y	U	I	B	X	C	V	B
M	C	S	E	A	G	H	M	K	N	O	H	P	K	O	N	M	A
H	O	O	J	A	L	C	V	O	L	E	S	O	U	L	U	S	H
W	V	B	M	B	L	M	E	P	T	Q	S	V	N	F	H	R	D
E	E	N	R	M	Z	F	X	C	V	H	W	S	G	O	O	H	M
R	T	M	T	U	I	B	N	M	A	S	E	K	L	Z	U	H	G
T	U	E	Y	W	O	T	D	F	G	H	E	R	C	V	S	R	R
Y	I	T	N	A	V	R	E	S	D	I	A	M	N	M	E	Q	H

5. __________ thy ________ and thy __________: that thy _____ may be ______ upon the _______ which the ______ thy _____ giveth thee.

6. Thou shalt not _____.

7. Thou shalt not ________ ____________.

8. Thou shalt not ______.

9. Thou shalt not _____ ________ _________ ___________ thy ☼___________.

10. Thou shalt not •_______ thy ☼____________'s _____, thou shalt not •_______ thy ☼____________'s _____, nor his ______________, nor his _______________, nor his ox, nor his ass, nor any thing that is thy ☼____________'s.

Answer: Divine _ _ _ _ _ _ _ _

TOGETHER FOREVER

[HIDDEN MESSAGE]

Beginning at the shaded square, draw a zigzag line from the top row to the bottom row. Do the same thing starting below the shaded square to complete the scripture. Use the bolded letters to find the final theme from *The Family: A Proclamation to the World*. Check page 168 for the reference.

The**r**efore	cleav**e**	a	his	le**a**ve	and	father	shall	his	**o**ne	an**d**
shall	shall	u**n**to	man	w**i**fe:	his	they	an**d**	be	mother	flesh.

Marriage between a man and a woman is __ __ __ __ __ __ __ __ of God.

UNITED IN PURPOSE

[CODE]

Each letter in the passage has been changed to a symbol. For example, s = ¶. Crack the code to find the scripture principle. Check page 168 for the reference and a hint.

% V Θ • § $ +→ √ Θ * % + + $ Θ § # ¶

↓ $ → ↓ + $ ¢ # → V, £ $ * % X ¶ $ • § $ z

¥ $ √ $ → Ω → V $ § $ % √ • % V Θ

→ V $ @ # V Θ, % V Θ Θ ¥ $ + • # V

√ # v § • $ → X ¶ V $ ¶ ¶; % V Θ • § $ √ $

¥ % ¶ V → ↓ → → √ % @ → V v • § $ @.

VOICE OF WARNING

[SCRIPTURE FIND]

Choose the correct bolded word for the following scriptures. Write the chosen word from each scripture above the corresponding number in the final passage to reveal the theme. Check page 168 for the reference and a hint.

1. O give thanks unto the [**Lord** or **God**] of gods: for his mercy endureth for ever. (Psalm 136:2)
2. Yea, verily I say unto you, in that day when the Lord shall come, he shall [**tell** or **reveal**] all things. (D&C 101:32)
3. For the Lord will judge [**those** or **his**] people, and he will repent himself concerning his servants. (Psalm 135:14)
4. If any man will do his [**will** or **part**], he shall know of the doctrine, whether it be of God, or whether I speak of myself. (John 7:17)
5. But thanks be to God, which giveth us the victory [**by** or **through**] our Lord Jesus Christ. (1 Corinthians 15:57)
6. And when they came thither to the hill, behold, a company of [**prophets** or **soldiers**] met him; and the Spirit of God came upon him, and he prophesied among them. (1 Samuel 10:10)

________ ________s ______ ________ ________ __________.

1 2 3 4 5 6

SCRIPTURE PUZZLERS

WISE IN THEIR OWN EYES

[CODE]

Each letter in the passage has been changed to a different letter. For example, P has been changed to N (n = p). Crack the code to find the scripture principle. Check page 169 for the reference and a hint.

Bjq diaj axqf axya oyss qgrs tjje, yie tjje qgrs; axya

nda eyhuiqzz kjh srtxa, yie srtxa kjh eyhuiqzz; axya

nda lraaqh kjh zbqqa, yie zbqqa kjh lraaqh!

WISE PURPOSE

[HIDDEN MESSAGE]

Cross off the letters J, Q, V, X, and Z to find the scripture. Check page 169 for the reference.

XJTXHJJEXNQJXVTVHQEVWJOJRXDOJQFVTXHEQZLORDJQCAZM

VEJUQNVZTOQMJE,QVSAQYIQQNQG,BQEJFOQRZXEIFOXQRMEDTZJHEX

QEQIJXNTXVHZVEBVELXXLVYIKXXNZEXJWTQHEXVE;AQXXNZVDBJEZF

JQOVRETHZOUZXCJAXMEVSTFZOVRTJHOVUVZTOQFVZTXXHVEWXOVJ

VVMBVISZAXJNCVTIFVJQIEZJDTZHEXVJE,AQXVNDXIOVQRDVAJZQINXEX

DTXHZEVZQEVVAPZRZOPZHQZEJTUJNXTQJOTHQXENJAQTIOQVQNJVXS.

NEW TESTAMENT PUZZLERS

A CITY SET ON A HILL

[MATCHING]

Match the reference with the key words for each scripture. Write the letter from the right column on the line with the corresponding number to find the final theme. Check page 169 for the reference and a hint.

1. 1 Corinthians 15:40–42	Repent, be baptized, and receive the Holy Ghost. (h)
2. Matthew 16:19	"If ye love me, keep my commandments." (o)
3. 2 Thessalonians 2:1–3	Your body is a temple. (n)
4. Matthew 28:19–20	Faith without works is dead. (s)
5. Revelation 20:12	Born of water and of the Spirit. (i)
6. Hebrews 12:9	The keys of the kingdom. (i)
7. John 14:15	The degrees of glory. (l)
8. James 2:17–18	Apostasy foretold. (g)
9. Acts 2:36–38	Teach and baptize all nations. (h)
10. John 3:5	Apostles and prophets help perfect the Saints. (e)
11. 1 Corinthians 6:19–20	Judged before God. (t)
12. Ephesians 4:11–12	God is the Father of our spirits. (s)

Let your __ __ __ __ __   __ __   __ __ __ __ __.
1 2 3 4 5   6 7   8 9 10 11 12

A HOUSE OF GOD

[LETTER CLUE]

Fill in the answer to each clue. Write the numbered letters from the answers above the corresponding numbers in the final scripture. If a word is repeated, it is marked with a symbol. Check page 169 for the reference and a hint.

1. Reading and analyzing to learn ___ ___ ___ ___ ___ ___ ___ ___
   14 31 13 43 46
2. Sexual purity ___ ___ ___ ___ ___ ___ ___ ___
   39 9 50 58 23
3. Information you gain in education ___ ___ ___ ___ ___ ___ ___ ___ ___
   34 3 33 22 45 38
4. The "good news" of Jesus Christ ___ ___ ___ ___ ___ ___
   24 30 53 17 47
5. Praying and showing respect for God ___ ___ ___ ___ ___ ___ ___ ___ ___ ___ ___
   26 42 25 54 29
6. A second witness of Jesus Christ ___ ___ ___ ___ ___ ___ ___ ___ ___ ___ ___ ___
   10 48 1 51 8 16
7. The act of following the laws of God ___ ___ ___ ___ ___ ___ ___ ___ ___
   35 55 6 44
8. The quality of being truthful and fair ___ ___ ___ ___ ___ ___ ___
   11 7 27 28 5
9. The power to use the priesthood ___ ___ ___ ___ ___ ___ ___ ___ ___
   37 40 20 32 56 52
10. Having great strength or influence ___ ___ ___ ___ ___ ___ ___ ___
    41 36 4 15 49 18
11. A sacred act performed with the priesthood ___ ___ ___ ___ ___ ___ ___ ___ ___
    21 12 57 2 19

What? ___ ___ ___ ___ ___ ___ ___ ___ ___ that your ♦___ ___ ___ ___ is the
1 2 3 4 5 6 7 8 9 10 11 12 13
___ ___ ___ ___ ___ ___ of the ___ ___ ___ ___ ___ ___ ___ ___ ___ which is in you, which ye
14 15 16 17 18 19 20 21 22 23 24 25 26 27 28
have of ♥___ ___ ___, and ye are not your ___ ___ ___? For ye are ___ ___ ___ ___ ___ ___ with a
29 30 31 32 33 34 35 36 37 38 39 40
___ ___ ___ ___ ___: therefore ___ ___ ___ ___ ___ ___ ___ ♥___ ___ ___ in your ♦___ ___ ___ ___, and in
41 42 43 44 45 46 47 48 49 50 51 52 29 30 31 10 11 12 13
your ___ ___ ___ ___ ___ ___, which are ♥___ ___ ___'s.
53 54 55 56 57 58 29 30 31

A SACRED GIFT

[WORD SEARCH]

Search forward, backward, up, down, and diagonally to find words and phrases that apply to 1 Corinthians 6:19–20. Unscramble the intersecting letters to find the final theme. Check page 170 for a hint.

F	H	K	O	U	T	E	Q	S	D	C	R	N	M	C	M
B	W	V	F	H	N	W	E	H	T	L	A	E	H	W	S
P	S	O	R	V	J	C	M	C	A	E	S	I	G	I	I
O	I	H	R	E	L	R	H	D	Z	A	W	F	J	Y	T
I	M	J	P	D	S	O	N	A	O	N	O	D	K	C	P
J	A	O	S	R	O	P	B	V	S	N	T	S	L	T	A
Y	G	I	R	S	L	F	E	L	E	T	H	T	R	I	B
H	E	P	E	E	A	R	W	C	I	L	I	P	M	U	K
T	O	U	N	T	C	U	V	I	T	E	R	T	N	P	L
G	F	R	N	P	I	U	C	G	S	H	O	L	Y	O	D
R	G	T	M	M	S	R	X	M	O	D	E	S	T	Y	E
W	O	R	T	H	Y	B	I	H	U	B	O	U	B	B	R
I	D	E	P	N	H	U	Z	P	H	T	P	M	V	N	C
D	S	K	O	B	P	O	K	J	S	Y	K	I	C	W	A
A	C	X	I	V	T	E	M	P	T	A	T	I	O	N	S

Your _ _ _ _ _   _ _   _ _ _ _ _.

ALL WILL LIVE AGAIN

[MATCHING]

Match the reference with the key words for each scripture. Write the letter from the right column on the line with the corresponding number to find the final theme. Check page 170 for the reference and a hint.

1. Matthew 11:28–30	The times of restitution. (R)
2. Matthew 22:36–39	A resurrected body has flesh and bones. (S)
3. Luke 24:36–39	Fruit of the Spirit. (E)
4. John 14:6	Scripture given for doctrine, reproof, and correction. (T)
5. John 17:3	The gospel is preached to the dead. (E)
6. Acts 3:19–21	I can do all things through Christ. (C)
7. Galatians 5:22–23	Knowing God and Jesus Christ is eternal life. (R)
8. Philippians 4:13	Come unto me. (R)
9. 2 Timothy 3:15–17	If you lack wisdom, ask God. (D)
10. 1 Peter 4:6	The way, the truth, and the life. (U)
11. James 1:5–6	Love the Lord, and love thy neighbor. (E)

In Christ shall all be __ __ __ __ __ __ __ __ __ __ __.
1 2 3 4 5 6 7 8 9 10 11

ALWAYS NEAR

[CODE]

Each letter in the passage has been changed to a symbol. For example, Q = &. Crack the code to find the scripture principle. Check page 170 for the reference and a hint.

% ~ < ♦ <   • ↑ @   < * ♈ ~ @ ↓ * ☼ ~ @   ♦ <   * $

X $ ♥ ☼ ↑ * ~ → ~ ♈   ↓ $ X   ♈ ~ & ♦ # ♈ ~ <

$ +   ♦ <.

ASCENSION FOR ALL

[SCRIPTURE FIND]

Fill in the missing words of the scripture by finding the correct word in each given hymn or scripture reference. If a word is repeated, it is marked with a symbol. Check page 170 for the reference and a hint.

But now is (♥Hymn #134, title) risen from the (●Hymn #5, vs. 4), and become the (Hymn #218, vs. 2) of them that slept. For since by (♠Hymn #29, title) came death, by (♠Hymn #29, title) came also the (Hymn #122, vs. 1) of the (●Hymn #5, vs. 4). For as in (Hymn #49, title) all die, even so in (♥Hymn #134, title) shall all be made (Hymn #79, vs. 3).

ASK TO KNOW

[CODE]

NEW TESTAMENT PUZZLERS

Each letter in the passage has been changed to the letter that comes after it in the alphabet. Crack the code to find the scripture principle. Check page 170 for the reference and a hint.

H p e   x j m m j o h m z   h j w f t   x j t e p n   u p

u i p t f   x i p   b t l   p g   I j n   j o   g b j u i.

BE BAPTIZED

[CODE]

Each letter in the passage has been changed to a different letter. For example, O has been changed to T (t = o). Crack the code to find the scripture principle. Check page 171 for the reference and a hint.

Lnoio zqornbns, Hnbmpv, hnbmpv, M ozv iqat adnn,

Ngxnfa z wzq en etbq ty rzanb zqs ty adn Ofmbma,

dn xzqqta nqanb mqat adn cmqjstw ty Jts.

BE NOT AFRAID

[SCRIPTURE FIND]

Fill in the missing words of the scripture by finding the correct word in each given hymn or scripture reference. If a word is repeated, it is marked with a symbol. Check page 171 for the reference and a hint.

And as they thus spake, (Hymn #141, title) himself stood (Hymn #108, vs. 3, 4 words) them, and saith unto them, (Hymn #98, vs. 1) be unto you. But they were (Philippians 1:28) and (Deuteronomy 7:21), and supposed that they had seen a (Hymn #179, vs. 1). And he said unto them, Why are ye (Hymn #277, vs. 3)? and why do (Hymn #169, vs. 1) arise in your (Hymn #115, vs. 1)? Behold my (Hymn #191, vs. 2) and my (Hymn #191, vs. 2), that it is I (Hymn #129, vs. 1): handle me, and see; for a spirit hath not (Hymn #175, vs. 2) and bones, as ye see me have.

BOUNTEOUS BLESSINGS

[WORD SEARCH]

Search forward, backward, up, down, and diagonally to find the words and phrases missing from the scripture below. Check page 171 for the reference and a hint.

K	Y	L	S	T	F	A	I	T	H	Q	T	C	M
S	F	A	R	S	H	J	N	Q	P	E	S	G	E
G	O	O	D	N	E	S	S	H	M	W	C	Y	D
R	Q	R	M	P	F	N	O	P	T	V	O	B	T
C	S	S	E	N	K	E	E	M	S	J	R	P	I
P	J	B	G	D	P	R	Q	L	K	R	U	S	R
E	C	A	E	P	A	T	V	U	T	O	E	N	I
H	M	S	E	N	C	I	B	M	O	N	G	K	P
T	G	V	C	E	Y	U	R	G	F	D	E	L	S
D	O	E	B	J	L	R	J	S	C	H	Z	G	A
L	O	N	G	S	U	F	F	E	R	I	N	G	F

But the _ _ _ _ _ of the _ _ _ _ _ _ is _ _ _ _, _ _ _, _ _ _ _ _,

_ _ _ _ _ _ _ _ _ _ _ _ _ _, _ _ _ _ _ _ _ _ _ _ _ _, _ _ _ _ _ _ _ _ _,

_ _ _ _ _, _ _ _ _ _ _ _ _ _, _ _ _ _ _ _ _ _ _ _ _ _ _: against such there is no law.

DIVINE GUIDANCE

[CROSSWORD]

Use the clues given inside the passage to find the answers to the crossword and complete the scripture. Some words may be repeated. Check page 171 for the reference and a hint.

1 2 3 4 5 6 7 8 9 10 B

If any of you lack [7↓ intelligence] ______________, let him ask of [8↓ Heavenly Father] __________, that giveth to all men [3↓ generously; abundantly] __________________, and [10→ blameth] ____________ not; and it shall be given [5→ opposite of her] __________. But let him ask in [1→ trust in something unseen] ___________, nothing [7→ undecided] _______________. For he that wavereth is like a [9→ rolling water] _______________ of the [4↓ body of salt water] ________ driven with the [6↓ air current] ______________ and [2↓ thrown; flung] _______________.

EVERLASTING BLESSING

[HIDDEN MESSAGE]

Beginning at the shaded square, draw a zigzag line from the top row to the bottom row. Do the same thing starting below the shaded square to complete the scripture. Use the bolded letters to find the final theme. Check page 171 for the reference.

And	onl**y**	**is**	God,	e**t**ernal,	Jesus	they	wh**o**m	know	has**t**	
the	this	true	lif**e**	and	that	Chri**s**t,	**m**ight	thou	thee	se**n**t.

_ _ _ _ _ _ _ _ _

FIND REFUGE IN ME

[HIDDEN MESSAGE]

Follow the code to find the corresponding words. Write the words on the spaces to discover a scripture with a great blessing. Some words may be used more than once. Fill in the words at the bottom of the puzzle to find the principle of the scripture. Check page 171 for the reference.

	1	2	3	4	5	6	7	8
A	give	for	learn	burden	is	heavy	am	Take
B	labour	Come	Jesus	I	yoke	burdens	upon	in
C	heart	souls	shall	meek	that	For	easy	me
D	all	lowly	are	Christ	light	you	of	your
E	laden	ye	rest	my	unto	will	find	and

Begin

B2 ________ E6________ A2________ E5________

E5 ________ A1________ B4________ D8________

C8 ________, D6________ A7________ C2________.

D1________ E3________. C4________ C6________

E2 ________ A8________ E8________ E4________

C5________ E4________ D2________ B5________

B1________ B5________ B8________ A5________

E8________ B7________ C1________: C7________,

D3________ D6________, E8________ E8________

A6________ E8________ E2________ E4________

E1________, A3________ C3________ A4________

E8________ D7 ________ E7________ A5________

B4________ C8________; E3________ D5________.

If we come unto B3 ________ D4 ________, He will ease our B6 ________.

FOREVER BOUND

[MATCHING]

Fill in the blanks of the scripture with the phrases listed. Check page 171 for the reference.

shall not prevail against it

which is in heaven

thou shalt loose on earth

That thou art Peter

loosed in heaven

the keys of the kingdom of heaven

in heaven

Thou art the Christ

But whom say ye that I am

hath not revealed it unto thee

I will build my church

Blessed art thou, Simon Bar-jona

the living God

bind on earth

He saith unto them, _____ ________ _____ ____ _______ ___ ____? And Simon Peter
answered and said, _____ ____ ____ _________, the Son of ____ _______ ____. And
Jesus answered and said unto him, _________ ____ _____, _______ __________:
for flesh and blood ______ _____ __________ ____ ______ ______, but my
Father ________ ____ ____ ____________. And I say also unto thee,
____ ____ ____ ______, and upon this rock __ _____ _______ ____ _______;
and the gates of hell ______ ____ _________ _________ ___. And I will give
unto thee ____ ______ ___ ____ _________ ___ _________: and whatsoever
thou shalt ______ ____ _______ shall be bound ___ _________: and whatsoever
_____ _____ ________ ___ ______ shall be _________ ___ _________.

GOOD NEWS FOR ALL

[HIDDEN MESSAGE]

Starting at the marked word, follow the directions to choose the words on the table. Write the words in the spaces to reveal a scripture with a great blessing. Some words may be used more than once. The two unused words reveal an additional truth about this scripture. Check page 171 for the reference.

are	preached	men	for	the	but	taught
be	★For	dead	God	according	everyone	to
gospel	judged	in	them	live	was	they
cause	that	might	also	this	spirit	flesh

Begin ★ ____________

Right 2, up 1 ____________

Down 3, right 1 ____________

Left 4 ____________

Up 1, right 5 ____________

Up 2, left 1 ____________

Left 4, down 2 ____________

Up 2, right 1 ____________

Down 3, right 2 ____________

Right 3, up 2 ____________

Down 1, left 3 ____________

Left 2, down 1 ____________

Up 3, left 1 ____________

Down 1, right 2 ____________,

Down 2, left 1 ____________

Right 5, up 1 ____________

Left 4, down 1 ____________

Up 2, left 2 ____________

Right 1, down 1 ____________

Right 3, up 1 ____________

Right 2 ____________

Up 1, left 4 ____________

Down 2 ____________

Up 2, right 2 ____________

Right 2, down 3 ____________,

Up 3, left 1 ____________

Down 2, left 1 ____________

Up 1 ____________

Right 2 ____________

Left 3 ____________

Down 1, left 1 ____________

Up 2, right 2 ____________

Right 1, down 3 ________.

HEAVENLY KINGDOMS

[CROSSWORD]

Use the clues given to find answers to the crossword. Place the answers on the corresponding spaces in the scripture on the next page. Some words may be repeated. Check page 172 for the reference and a hint.

Across

1. The highest glory of heaven
5. The middle glory of heaven
9. Reuniting of spirit and body
10. Lifted up
12. In addition
15. Physical decay
16. A crescent shaped (at times) heavenly body
18. Varieth

Down

2. A twinkling heavenly body
3. One more
4. The lowest glory of heaven
6. The majesty of God
7. Deprived of life
8. Being free from physical decay
11. Far away suns; form constellations
13. A shining heavenly body
14. Planted (like seeds)
17. Single, unit

There are also (1) ________________ bodies, and bodies (5) ________________: but the (6) ________ of the (1) ________________ is (17) ______ and the (6) ________ of the (5)________________ is (3) __________. There is (17) ______ (6) ________ of the (13) ________, and (3) ____________ (6) ____________ of the (16) __________, and (3) ________________ (6) ______________ of the (11) __________: for one (2) _______ (18) ____________ from (3) __________ (2) ______ in (6) ________. So (12) _______ is the (9) __________________ of the (7) _______. It is (14) _______ in (15) ___________; it is (10) ________ in (8) __________________.

HELP FROM ON HIGH

[HIDDEN MESSAGE]

Cross off the letters B, F, J, K, P, and V to find the scripture. Check page 172 for the reference.

JKPIVBCJJABKNKPVDVOJKBVAKPKLPLJFPBTKBVHFBVIVPBNBFBGVBFS

VPBVJKJVTBJFVHVRVPBOBJKVUVBGFBHKKBCPBPVHVKKVRJFIVSBJFTP

WFFHBJIKVCVVBHKFJBKSJJKPTVKVRBPEVBFNVBGPJTKHBPJEKBBNVE

KJPTFKHBJKMVBEK.

HOW CAN WE KNOW THE WAY?

[CODE]

Each word in the passage has been changed to numbers. Solve the mathematical equations to match the words with the numbers. Some words may be used more than once. Check page 172 for the reference and a hint.

12 10 6 8, 2 14 15 16, 15 21, 9 15 32:

11 18 25 6 15 24, 30 33 45.

life	8x4
the	3x5
Jesus	3x4
no	5+6
and	3x3
I	2x1
cometh	5x5
am	2x7
truth	3x7
him	4+4
unto	2x3
me	9x5
by	11x3
saith	5+5
but	6x5
man	9+9
way	2x8
Father	8x3

JUDGMENT DAY

[CODE]

Each letter in the passage has been changed to a different letter. For example, W has been changed to V (v = w). Crack the code to find the scripture principle. Check page 172 for the reference and a hint.

B z e T q b v o j g e g b e, q r b c c b z e x f g b o, q o b z e y g a n f g X n e;

b z e o j g y n n u q v g f g n h g z g e: b z e b z n o j g f y n n u v b q n h g z g e,

v j t m j t q o j g y n n u n a c t a g: b z e o j g e g b e v g f g d s e x g e n s o

n a o j n q g o j t z x q v j t m j v g f g v f t o o g z t z o j g y n n u q,

b m m n f e t z x o n o j g t f v n f u q.

PERFECTED STATE

[WORD SCRAMBLE]

Unscramble the words in the passage below to reveal the scripture principle. The first two words have been done for you. Check page 172 for the reference and a hint.

JESUS CHRIST SI A RUECRETEDSR GEBIN. A RUECRETEDSR DBYO SI A DBYO FO SFEHL NAD SEBNO.

PREPARE FOR BLESSINGS

[LETTER DROP]

Discover the following scripture by dropping the letters at the top into the correct boxes directly below them. Read the scripture left to right. Some words have been done for you. The highlighted spaces all contain the same letter. Check page 172 for the reference and a hint.

~~O~~ R R	E E ~~F~~ R	B C E M P	A E I P R T	E E H I P S	E N P S T V	A E I T	A H O R S	E M N N O T	C H L	E E ~~F~~ ~~O~~ U Y	~~F~~ ~~O~~ S	~~A~~ G G ~~R~~	H I ~~N~~ S T	~~D~~ F I O O T	H N S T	E S T
■											■	A	N	D	■	■
■	■								■	F	O	R	■			
									■	O	F	■				
■	■								■			■			■	■
							■				■					■
O	F	■				■					■					.

RESTITUTION FORETOLD

[MATCHING]

Match the words in the left column with the words in the right column to complete each phrase of the scripture. Write the letter from the right column on the line with the corresponding number to find the final theme. Check page 172 for the reference.

Repent ye therefore, and be ________________,	unto you (E)
that your sins may be ___________ _______,	must receive (C)
when the times of __________________	blotted out (R)
shall come from the ____________ ___ ___ ______;	Jesus Christ (H)
And he shall send ___________ __________,	holy prophets (E)
which before was preached ________ _______:	converted (P)
whom the heaven ________ ___________	presence of the Lord (P)
until the times of _____________ ___ ____ ________,	refreshing (O)
which God hath spoken by the mouth of all his	began (S)
_________ ____________	restitution of all things (I)
since the world ___________.	

___ ___ ___ ___ ___ ___ ___ ___ ___ ___

1 2 3 4 5 6 7 8 9 10

SHINE ON!

[CROSSWORD]

Use the clues given to find answers to the crossword. The highlighted squares contain the same letter. Place the answers on the corresponding spaces in the scripture. Some words may be repeated. Check page 173 for the reference and a hint.

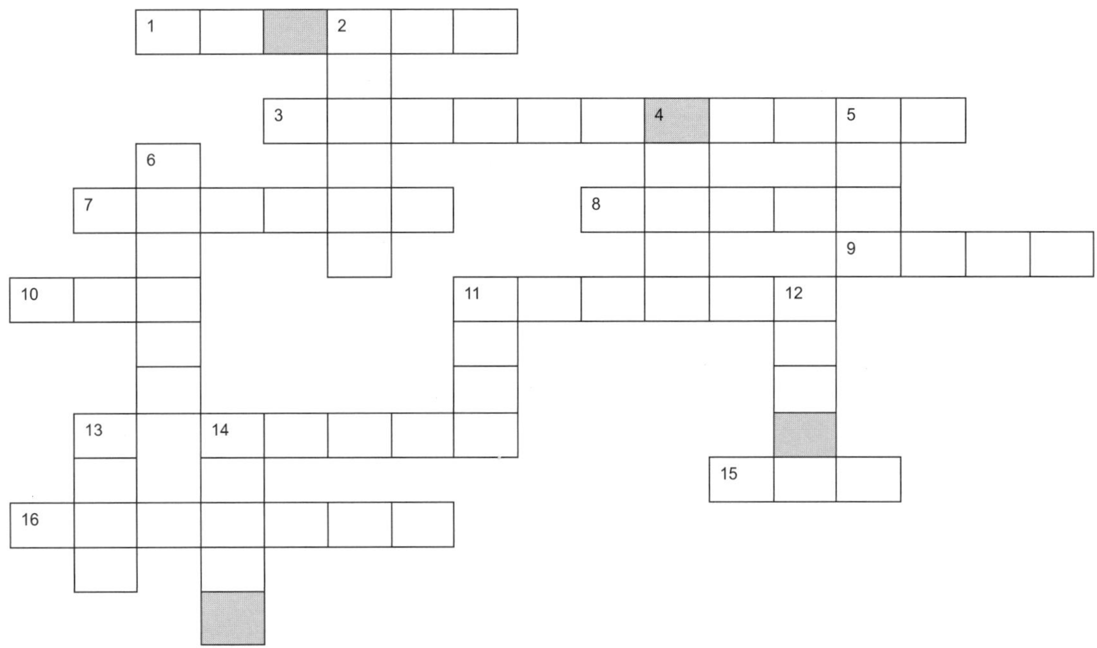

Across
1. Basketful, bundle
3. Holder of a wax shape that burns
7. He who created our spirits
8. Energy that helps you see
9. Possessive of *you*
10. Put away so it can't be found
11. Opposite of taketh
14. The earth and its people
15. Males
16. To honor and praise

Down
2. The place where God dwells
4. Glow, glimmer
5. Metropolis, large town
6. A wax shape with a wick
11. Opposite of bad
12. A structure where a family lives
13. Rounded, smaller than a mountain
14. Actions, doings

Ye are the (8→) ________ of the (14→) __________. A (5↓) __________ that is set on an (13↓) ______ cannot be (10→) _______. Neither do (15→) ______ (8→) __________ a (6↓) ___________, and put it under a (1→) __________, but on a (3→) _________________; and it (11→) ____________ (8→) __________ unto all that are in the (12↓) ___________. Let (9→) _______ (8→) _________ so (4↓) ___________ before (15→) _________, that they may see (9→) _________ (11↓) ________ (14↓) __________, and (16→) ___________ your (7→) ___________ which is in (2↓) ____________.

TEACH AND BAPTIZE

[LETTER DROP]

Discover the following scripture by dropping the letters at the top into the correct boxes directly below them. Read the scripture left to right. Some words have been done for you. The highlighted spaces all contain the same letter. Check page 173 for the reference and a hint.

A C O	B E L L N ~~O~~ O T W	A ~~F~~ G H H M N ~~O~~ O S ~~T~~ T W	~~A~~ A A D E E E ~~F~~ ~~H~~ M O T	A A ~~E~~ I I M ~~N~~ R ~~T~~ T Y	C ~~D~~ ~~H~~ N O O S ~~T~~ V Y	A D ~~E~~ E E E F ~~H~~ H H ~~I~~ N O	~~E~~ E E I M ~~N~~ O S T V	A D E E F L N ~~T~~ T V	A A B E G ~~H~~ H L N S ~~T~~ W Y	A C E E ~~H~~ I L O R T Y	~~E~~ G H H N O P R T T U	E E H H H I N T T U W	~~A~~ A E F H I N O O R T	~~A~~ A H I L M ~~N~~ O O R S Y Z	~~A~~ A ~~D~~ I L L M ~~N~~ N O R T	~~D~~ D E E G ~~N~~ N ~~T~~ T U V	~~D~~ E G ~~H~~ ~~O~~ O S	~~E~~ ~~F~~
■	■			■			■									,	■	■
■	■	■	A	N	D	■						■		░	░	■	■	■
■							,	■										■
■					■	I	N	■	T	H	E	■					■	■
■	O	F	■	T	H	E	■						,	■	A	N	D	■
■	■	O	F	■	T	H	E	■			,	■	A	N	D	■	O	F
■	■	T	H	E	■			░		■					:	■	■	■
■	■									■					■			■
							■		░	░	■							■
■											■		■					■
									■			:	■	A	N	D,	■	■
■	░	,	■		■			■					■				■	■
	░			,	■					■					■	T	H	E
■				■			■	T	H	E	■				░	.	■	■

Amen.

SCRIPTURE PUZZLERS

THE GOOD FIGHT

[SCRIPTURE FIND]

Find the missing words of each scripture. Write the found word from each scripture above the corresponding number in the final passage to reveal the theme. Check page 173 for the reference.

1. Wherefore, by (1) ______ was the law of Moses given. But in the gift of his Son (2) _______ God prepared a more excellent way; and it is by faith that it hath been fulfilled. (Ether 12:11)
2. And there were great and marvelous (3) ______ wrought by the disciples of Jesus, insomuch that they did heal the sick, and raise the (4) ______, and cause the lame to walk, and the blind to receive their sight. (4 Nephi 1:5)
3. And blessed are they because of their exceeding faith in the words (5) ______ which thou hast spoken unto them. (Mosiah 26:16)
4. And lo, he cometh unto his own, that salvation might come unto the children of men even through faith on his name; and even after all this they shall consider him a (6) _______, and (7) _______ that he hath a devil, and shall scourge him, and shall crucify him. (Mosiah 3:9)
5. Fight the good fight of faith, lay hold on eternal life, whereunto thou art also called, and (8)_______ professed a good profession before many witnesses. (1 Timothy 6:12)
6. Howbeit when he, the Spirit of truth, is come, he will guide you into all truth: for he shall not speak of himself; but whatsoever he shall hear, that shall he speak: and he will (9) ___ you things to come. (John 16:13)
7. Let us hold fast the profession of our faith (10) _________ wavering. (Hebrews 10:23)
8. And when he saw their faith, he said unto him, Man, thy sins are forgiven (11) _____. (Luke 5:20)

Even so (1) _________, if it (2) _______ not (3) __________, is (4) ________ , being (5) _________. Yea, a (6) ______ may (7) _____, Thou (8) _________ (1) _________, and I have (3) _________: (9) _________ me thy (1)_________ (10) ______________ thy (3) _______, and I will (9) _______ (11) _______ my (1) _________ by my (3) _________.

THE GREATEST TWO

[HIDDEN MESSAGE]

Solve the word puzzles in the passage below to complete the scripture. Some words may be repeated. Check page 173 for the reference.

(Mask – k + water – wa), which is the great (comic – ic + salamander – sala – er + meant – a) in the law? Jesus said unto him, Thou shalt (loan – an + velvet – lvet) the Lord thy God with all thy (heaven – ven + cart – ca), and with all thy (soup – p + l), and with all thy (mint – t + d). This is the (film – lm + roast – oa) and (green – en + cat – c) commandment. And the (seed – ed + opposite of pro + do – o) is like unto it, Thou shalt love thy (bone – bo + fight – f – t + bone – ne + fur – f) as (moth – mo + myself – m).

THE REASON WE OBEY

[LETTER CLUE]

Fill in the answer to each clue. Write the numbered letters from the answers above the corresponding numbers in the final scripture. If a word is repeated, it is marked with a symbol. Check page 173 for the reference and a hint.

1. To give of yourself to help others __ __ __ __ __
   (28, 10, _, 7, 12)

2. Communication with Heavenly Father __ __ __ __ __ __
   (14, _, 21, 3, 25, _)

3. Baptism by water __ __ __ __ __ __ __ __ __
   (_, 19, 9, 4, _, _, 1, _, 26)

4. Degrees of glory __ __ __ __ __ __ __ __
   (11, _, 22, _, 23, 6, 15, _)

5. Beyond this life; no death __ __ __ __ __ __ __ __ __ __ __
   (_, 20, 24, 18, _, _, _, 5, _, _, 16)

6. Without blemish, like our Lord __ __ __ __ __ __ __
   (_, 8, _, 2, 13, 17, 27)

__ __   __ __   __ __ __ __   __ __, __ __ __ __   __ __
1 2   3 4   5 6 7 8   9 10   11 12 13 14   15 16

__ __ __ __ __ __ __ __ __ __ __ __.
17 18 19 20 21 22 23 24 25 26 27 28

THEIR TEACHINGS

[MISSING-LETTER WORDS]

Every other letter is missing from the words and phrases of Old Testament prophets and things they have taught or shown us by their lives. The letters are listed in alphabetical order below. If a word is repeated, it is marked with a symbol. Check page 173 for the reference and a hint.

I _ a _ a _ = _ r _ p _ e _ i _ d _f _ a _ i _ r

D _ n _ e _ = _ a _ o _ h _ a _ t _

M _ l _ c _ i = t _ t _ i _ g

A _ r _ h _ m = o _ e _ i _ n _ e

N _ a _ = _ r _ p _ r _

J _ c _ b = f _ i _ h _ u _ p _ t _ i _ r _ h

A _ a _ = _ l _ n _f _ a _ v _ t _ o _

M _ s _ s = c _ m _ a _ d _ e _ t _

S _ m _ e _ = _ e _ r _ n _ r _ v _ l _ t _ r

E _ i _ a _ = _ e _ l _ n _ p _ w _ r

J _ n _ h = m _ s _ i _ n _ r _ w _ r _

a a a a a a a a a a a a a a a a a a b b c c d d d e e e e e e e

e e e f f g h h h h h h h i i i i i i j k l l l l l l l m m m n n

n n o o o o o o o o o o o o o p p p r s s s s s s s s t u v w y

TO PERFECT US

[LETTER DROP]

Discover the following scripture by dropping the letters at the top into the correct boxes directly below them. Read the scripture left to right. Some words have been done for you. The highlighted spaces all contain the same letter. Check page 174 for the reference and a hint.

And he gave . . .

O	F	A	B	A	C	D	A	F	A	E	C	G	E	~~E~~	F	~~A~~	~~A~~	~~D~~	~~D~~
S	O	~~H~~	E	~~H~~	D	E	A	F	F	I	F	H	E	F	S	~~A~~	~~A~~	~~D~~	~~D~~
	S	M	E	M	~~E~~	E	C	I	G	I	G	H	~~H~~	I	S	F	~~E~~	~~E~~	~~E~~
	~~T~~	P	E	N	E	E	E	N	I	N	L	I	O	O	S	~~H~~	~~H~~	~~H~~	K
		S	~~E~~	O	E	H	I	O	N	O	N	L	R	S	~~T~~	~~T~~	~~N~~	~~N~~	
		T	I	O	E	S	M	P	O	R	P	O	R	S		T	~~N~~	~~N~~	
			O	O	F	V		P	O	S	S	O	R	T		W	O	R	
			S	R	M	Y		P	R	S	T	T	R	T			O	R	
			S		M			R	S		T	~~T~~	S	Y			~~T~~		
			~~T~~		T			T	Y										

■	■	░			,	■				░				░ ;	■	A	N	D	■
■	■	■	░			,	■								░ ;	■	A	N	D
░			,	■									░		░ ;	■	A	N	D
■	■	■	░			,	■			░				░	■	A	N	D	■
■	■								░ ;	■				■	T	H	E	■	■
■	■											■			■	T	H	E	■
■	░					░ ,	■				■	T	H	E	■				
		■	T	H	E	■					░			,	■				■
■	T	H	E	■									■			■	T	H	E
■	■	■					■			■					░	.	■	■	■

WALK IN THE SPIRIT

[CROSSWORD]

Use the clues below to determine the words that apply to the scripture found in Galatians 5:22–23. The highlighted area shows what we will inherit as we apply the words of the theme to our lives. Check page 174 for a hint.

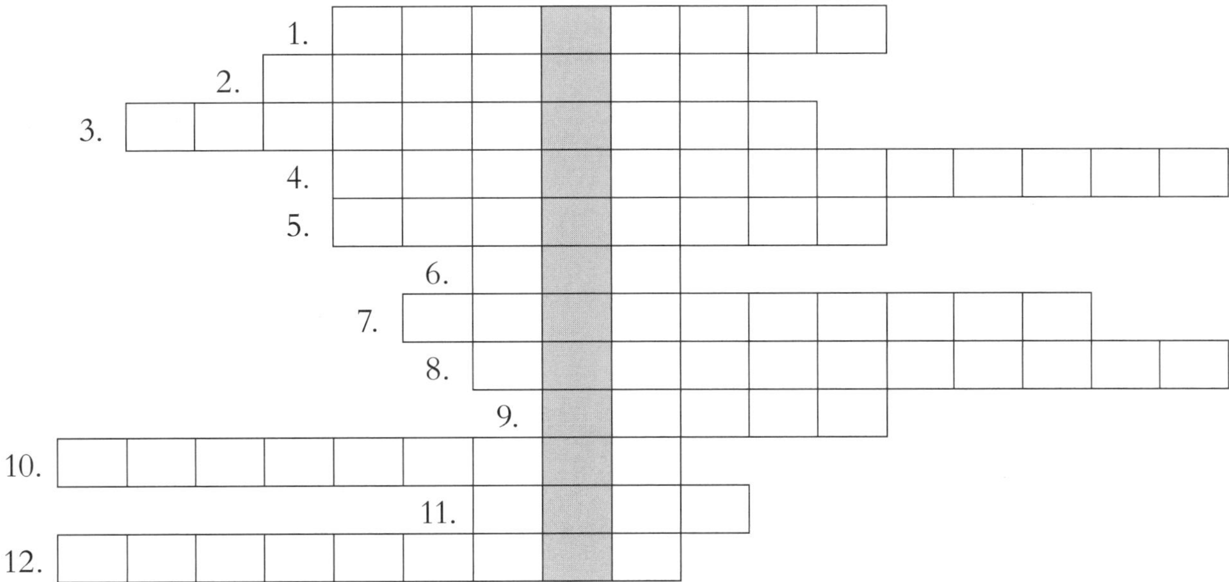

1. Lowliness of heart; humility
2. The pure love of Christ
3. Tenderness
4. Enduring without complaint
5. Benevolence, loving
6. "Men are, that they might have _____." (2 Nephi 2:25)
7. Moderation, restraint
8. To pardon or be pardoned
9. Hope in things not seen
10. Information that is obtained
11. The greatest commandment requires this
12. Thankfulness

WHAT SHALL WE DO?

[WORD SEARCH]

Search forward, backward, up, down, and diagonally to find the words and phrases missing from the scripture below. If a word is repeated, it is marked with a symbol. Unscramble the intersecting letters to find the final theme. Check page 174 for the reference and a hint.

A	D	G	I	R	E	M	I	S	S	I	O	N	J	E	N
E	R	T	Y	U	P	E	C	O	A	J	S	Y	A	O	W
H	H	E	A	R	T	N	R	R	F	U	E	C	I	F	O
D	G	O	D	E	T	R	N	U	U	A	B	S	C	P	A
J	E	I	L	S	G	K	E	W	E	C	Z	T	U	A	N
V	U	R	I	Y	C	V	R	P	N	F	I	O	T	S	T
B	S	R	D	Q	G	I	A	S	E	P	X	F	B	I	F
N	H	O	R	W	J	H	P	P	G	N	I	P	I	V	A
C	I	S	A	A	H	F	O	S	D	G	T	R	S	E	P
R	G	I	E	T	L	C	S	S	E	D	K	I	R	I	D
T	Y	G	H	R	F	G	T	B	T	I	R	E	A	K	T
A	S	S	U	R	E	D	L	Y	R	E	B	O	E	Y	G
P	N	F	I	Y	C	H	E	C	V	N	B	G	L	E	V
D	G	K	O	U	A	J	S	P	R	I	C	K	E	D	E
L	P	E	D	E	Z	I	T	P	A	B	R	I	T	Y	S

Therefore let all the house of _ _ _ _ _ _ _ know _ _ _ _ _ _ _ _ _ _ _ _, that _ _ _ hath made that same ♥_ _ _ _ _, whom ye have _ _ _ _ _ _ _ _ _ _ _, both _ _ _ _ and ♦ _ _ _ _ _ _ _. Now when they _ _ _ _ _ this, they were _ _ _ _ _ _ _ in their _ _ _ _ _, and said unto Peter and to the rest of the _ _ _ _ _ _ _ _, _ _ _ and brethren, what shall we do? Then Peter said unto them, _ _ _ _ _ _ _, and be _ _ _ _ _ _ _ _ every one of you in the name of ♥_ _ _ _ _ ♦_ _ _ _ _ _ for the _ _ _ _ _ _ _ _ _ _ _ of sins, and ye shall receive the _ _ _ _ of the _ _ _ _ _ _ _ _ _.

Theme: _ _ _ _ _w _ _ _

WHEN WILL HE COME?

[MATCHING]

Fill in the blanks of the scripture with the phrases listed. Check page 174 for the reference.

beseech you, brethren

deceive you by any means

nor by letter as from us

be revealed, the son of perdition

Christ is at hand

shall not come

neither by spirit

a falling away first

together unto him

our Lord Jesus Christ

shaken in mind

Now we ________ ______, __________, by the coming of____ _____ ______ ______, and by our gathering _______ ____ _____, That ye be not soon ______ ___ _____, or be troubled, _______ ___ ______, nor by word, _____ ____ ________ ____ ______ ____, as that the day of______ ___ ___ _____. Let no man _______ ____ ___ ____ ______: for that day ______ ____ _____, except there come __ ______ _____ _____, and that man of sin ___ ________, ____ ____ ___ ________.

WHOM THE LORD LOVES

[SCRIPTURE FIND]

Choose the correct bolded word for the following scriptures. Write the chosen word from each scripture above the corresponding number in the final passage to reveal the theme. Check page 174 for the reference.

1. Moreover I will subdue all thine enemies. [**Wherefore** or **Furthermore**] I tell thee that the Lord will build thee an house. (1 Chronicles 17:10)
2. Whose are the [**fathers** or **brothers**] and of whom as concerning the [**body** or **flesh**] Christ came, who is over all, God blessed for ever. Amen. (Romans 9:5)
3. A servant will not be [**corrected** or **taught**] by words: for though he understand he will not answer. (Proverbs 29:19)
4. But last of all he sent unto them his son, saying, They will [**respect** or **reverence**] my son. (Matthew 21:37)
5. A good name is [**rather** or **more**] to be chosen than great riches, and loving favour rather than silver and gold. (Proverbs 22:1)
6. O ye, my people, lift up your heads and be comforted; for behold, the time is at hand, or is not far distant, when we shall no longer be in [**bondage** or **subjection**] to our enemies, notwithstanding our many strugglings, which have been in vain; yet I trust there remaineth an effectual struggle to be made. (Mosiah 7:18)
7. But, behold, my Beloved Son, which was my Beloved and Chosen from the beginning, said unto me—[**Lord** or **Father**], thy will be done, and the glory be thine forever. (Moses 4:2)
8. Behold, it has been made known unto me by an angel, that the [**bodies** or **spirits**] of all men, as soon as they are departed from this mortal body, yea, the spirits of all men, whether they be good or evil, are taken home to that God who gave them life. (Alma 40:11)
9. And all other principles of the gospel that were necessary for them to know in order to qualify themselves that they might be judged according to men in the flesh, but [**live** or **make holy**] according to God in the spirit. (D&C 138:34)

(1) ____________________ we have had (2) __________ of our (2) _______ which (3) _______ us, and we gave them (4) ______________: shall we not much (5) _________ be in (6)____________ unto the (7) ____________ of (8) ____________, and (9) _________?

WITH ALL THY HEART

[WORD SCRAMBLE]

Unscramble the words listed below. Place the unscrambled words on the correct lines in the passage to reveal how we can love God, which applies to John 14:15. If a word is repeated, it is marked with a symbol. Check page 174 for a hint.

arceg	thigm
veol	digusnolsen
hnrsgett	repow
frceetp	deprcefet
ndim	

Yea, come unto Christ, and be _ _ _ _ _ _ _ _ _ in him, and deny yourselves of all ♠_ _ _ _ _ _ _ _ _ _ _; and if ye shall deny yourselves of all ♠_ _ _ _ _ _ _ _ _ _ _, and _ _ _ _ God with all your _ _ _ _ _, _ _ _ _ and _ _ _ _ _ _ _ _, then is his ♥ _ _ _ _ _ sufficient for you, that by his ♥ _ _ _ _ _ ye may be ♦ _ _ _ _ _ _ _ in Christ; and if by the ♥ _ _ _ _ _ of God ye are ♦ _ _ _ _ _ _ _ in Christ, ye can in nowise deny the _ _ _ _ _ of God. (Moroni 10:32)

WORDS OF INSPIRATION

[WORD SCRAMBLE]

Unscramble the words in passage below to reveal the scripture. Check page 174 for the reference.

And that from a (dcilh) _____ thou hast known the (yohl) _____ (iurstserpc) ___________, which are able to make thee (iwes) ________ unto (avaonslti) ______________ through faith which is in Christ Jesus. All (ruscteipr) _________ is given by (npinoitasir) ____________ of God, and is (rfaebpoitl) _______________ for doctrine, for (ropofer) ______________, for (onicrtroec) ________________, for (conitrunsti) _______________ in righteousness: That the man of God may be (cperfte)____________, throughly (ednfuihsr) ____________ unto all good (roksw) ___________.

BOOK OF MORMON PUZZLERS

A PARTICLE

[LETTER CLUE]

Fill in the answer to each clue. Write the numbered letters from the answers above the corresponding numbers in the final scripture. If a word is repeated, it is marked with a symbol. Check page 175 for the reference and a hint.

1. Feeling of pain from sin _ _ _ _ _ _ _ _ _
   51 39 1 18 8 22
2. Action to develop and sustain faith _ _ _ _ _ _ _ _
   47 52 41 15
3. What comes from sincere repentance _ _ _ _ _ _ _ _ _ _ _
   35 56 3 29 11 32
4. Opposite of falsehood _ _ _ _ _
   9 37 42 5
5. He who redeems us _ _ _ _ _   _ _ _ _ _ _
   38 57 31 16 4
6. Works, something done in faith _ _ _ _ _ _
   40 55 49 54
7. A gift for members of the Church _ _ _ _   _ _ _ _ _
   10 23 28 43 45 20
8. Going after, in His footsteps _ _ _ _ _ _ _ _ _
   6 25 12 24 48
9. The act of keeping the commandments _ _ _ _ _ _ _ _ _
   36 53 27 58 19
10. To bear trials calmly, without complaint _ _ _ _ _ _ _
    14 2 13 50
11. To whom we pray _ _ _ _ _ _
    17 7 30 44 33
12. Continue to obey _ _ _ _
    21 34 26 46

And now as I said concerning _1 _2 _3 _4 _5—_6 _7 _8 _9 _10 is _11 _12 _13 to have a _14 _15 _16 _17 _18 _19 _20 _21 _22 _23 _24 _25 _26 _27 _28 _29 of things; _30 _31 _32 _33 _34 _35 _36 _37 _38 if ye have _39 _40 _41 _42 _43 ye _44 _45 _46 _47 for things which are _48 _49 _50 _51 _52 _53 _54, which are _55 _56 _57 _58.

BOOK OF MORMON PUZZLERS

AGENCY

[MATCHING]

Fill in the blanks of the scripture with the phrases listed. Write the corresponding word in the blanks on the right to complete a sentence that reads vertically. Check page 175 for the reference.

death (Savior)

like unto himself (Christ)

liberty and eternal life (follow)

which are expedient unto man (will)

according to the flesh (I)

power of the devil (Jesus)

Mediator of all men (my)

Wherefore, men are free ________________________________; ______

and all things are given them ________________________________. ______

And they are free to choose ________________________________, ______

through the great ______________________________________, ______

or to choose captivity and ________________________________, ______

according to the captivity and ________________________________; ______

for he seeketh that all men might be miserable ____________________. ______

BE OBEDIENT

[HIDDEN MESSAGE]

Follow the code to find the corresponding words. Write the words on the spaces to discover a scripture with a great blessing. Some words may be used more than once. Check page 175 for the reference.

	A	B	C	D	E	F	G	H	J	K
1	go	Lord	I	commanded	no	unto	the	for	said	of
2	men	things	which	children	father	commandeth	he	they	prepare	which
3	unto	that		know	may	commandments	will	way	giveth	accomplish
4	shall	them	a	my	do	Nephi	thing	hath	save	and

And it came to pass . . .

B3_____ E4________ B3________ J4________ K3________

C1________, G1________ G1________ G2________ G1________

F4________, B2________ B1________ A4________ G4________

J1________ K2________ J3________ J2________ C2________

A3________ G1________ E1________ C4________ G2________

D4________ B1________ F3________ H3________ F2________

E2________: H4________ F1________ H1________ B4________.

C1________ D1________, G1________ B4________

G3________ H1________ D2________ B3________

A1________ C1________ K1________ H2________

K4________ D3________ A2________, E3________

SCRIPTURE PUZZLERS

BE TEACHABLE

[WORD SEARCH]

Search forward, backward, up, down, and diagonally to find the words and phrases missing from the scripture below. If a word is repeated, it is marked with a symbol. Check page 175 for the reference and a hint.

B	N	F	J	I	P	W	K	L	H	N	A	T	U	R	A	L	M	A	N	K	X	E	M	R
A	E	T	T	B	I	M	P	E	I	C	U	F	C	D	B	S	D	Q	A	L	K	B	R	C
S	E	N	E	M	Y	T	O	G	O	D	M	R	A	F	K	J	S	U	N	Y	L	U	Z	H
C	L	Q	Z	R	N	S	G	F	A	L	L	O	F	A	D	A	M	W	B	S	C	I	E	A
K	U	D	W	V	Y	O	V	O	B	D	I	Y	C	U	N	S	H	Y	K	L	V	R	N	F
U	C	F	X	J	S	N	U	M	D	T	J	B	T	R	G	D	E	T	Z	D	H	E	X	O
V	H	I	Y	E	M	F	O	R	E	V	E	R	C	A	M	X	S	Q	I	O	J	G	Q	A
Y	R	S	N	A	S	H	L	Y	S	E	J	X	Z	R	T	K	M	J	S	W	B	C	E	Y
J	M	C	G	X	A	B	K	T	Z	A	K	F	D	N	Y	P	A	H	X	F	E	T	L	V
Z	E	N	T	I	C	I	N	G	S	O	F	T	H	E	H	O	L	Y	S	P	I	R	I	T
D	K	O	B	E	V	W	V	G	Q	R	E	Q	L	D	L	A	C	J	N	W	A	M	S	N
I	N	X	D	Y	U	F	S	H	E	J	M	O	C	I	V	H	E	P	U	E	G	O	R	J
B	E	C	O	M	E	T	H	A	S	A	I	N	T	D	T	F	M	R	X	B	L	A	U	H
X	A	T	O	N	E	M	E	N	T	O	F	C	H	R	I	S	T	T	H	E	L	O	R	D
T	K	C	V	I	A	U	L	B	B	E	C	O	M	E	T	H	A	S	A	C	H	I	L	D
G	H	S	U	B	M	I	S	S	I	V	E	Z	N	I	A	X	K	H	V	J	M	E	E	K
A	M	R	B	N	Z	A	H	T	G	A	M	H	U	M	B	L	E	C	Y	Y	H	A	J	S
O	L	N	A	D	Q	D	S	P	R	B	A	O	X	U	E	S	L	Q	Z	E	B	O	P	L
Z	P	A	T	I	E	N	T	G	F	U	L	L	O	F	L	O	V	E	M	I	A	C	T	H
S	F	Y	G	A	T	K	H	W	L	V	X	M	B	P	Z	T	L	F	Q	D	W	V	B	G
N	M	P	R	E	K	U	B	A	I	C	D	A	J	G	H	A	L	N	S	X	U	K	Y	F
R	H	S	X	G	Y	C	W	I	L	L	I	N	G	T	O	S	U	B	M	I	T	P	A	E

For the ______ _____ is an _____ __ _____, and has been from the ____ ___ _____, and will be, ______ and ever, unless he yields to the ________ __ ___ _____ ______, and putteth off the natural man and ______ __ _____ through the ________ ___ _______ ___ _____, and ______ __ __ _____, ________, ________, ________, ________, ____ __ ______, _______ __ ______ to all things which the Lord seeth fit to inflict upon him, even as a child doth submit to his father.

BE WISE

[LETTER CLUE]

Fill in the answer to each clue. Write the numbered letters from the answers above the corresponding numbers in the final scripture. If a word is repeated, it is marked with a symbol. Check page 175 for the reference and a hint.

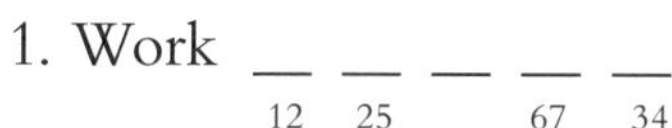

1. Work _ _ _ _ _ _
   12 25 67 34
2. Laboring in the Lord's vineyard _ _ _ _ _ _ _ _ _ _ _ _ _ _ _
   22 8 32 55 47 16 30 65 39 17 26
3. One who helps of their own free will _ _ _ _ _ _ _ _ _
   58 45 64 9 3 50
4. Chances to help others _ _ _ _ _ _ _ _ _ _ _ _ _
   21 63 57 1 18 36 24 54
5. Assisting, reaching out _ _ _ _ _ _ _ _ _ _ _
   29 44 51 66 7 20
6. The pure love of Christ _ _ _ _ _ _ _
   60 2 14 42 28 62
7. What you give _ _ _ _ _ _ _ _ _ _ _ _ _
   37 40 27 31 15 41 6 52 4
8. An act of kindness _ _ _ _ _ _ _ _ _ _ _
   49 56 38 46 33 13
9. The act of pardoning and forgetting _ _ _ _ _ _ _ _ _ _ _
   43 10 59 35 5 11 19
10. Information gained from being educated _ _ _ _ _ _ _ _ _
    48 23 68 53 61

And behold, I tell you _ _ _ _ _ (1 2 3 4 5) _ _ _ _ _ _ (6 7 8 9 10 11) that ye may _ _ _ _ _ (12 13 14 15 16) _ _ _ _ _ _ (17 18 19 20 21 22); that ye may _ _ _ _ _ (23 24 25 26 27) _ _ _ _ (28 29 30 31) when ye are in the _ _ _ _ _ _ _ (32 33 34 35 36 37 38) of _ _ _ _ (39 40 41 42) _ _ _ _ _ _ (43 44 45 46 47 48) _ _ _ _ _ _ (49 50 51 52 53 54) ye are only in the _ _ _ _ _ _ _ (55 56 57 58 59 60 61) of _ _ _ _ (62 63 64 65) _ _ _ (66 67 68).

BECOMING STRONG

[MISSING-LETTER WORDS]

Every other letter is missing from the words in this scripture. The letters are listed in alphabetical order below. If a word is repeated, it is marked with a symbol. Check page 175 for the reference.

And if men _ o _ e ● _ n _ o ♠ _ e I will _ h _ w ● _ n _ o ♦ _ h _ m _ h _ i _ ~ w _ a _ n _ s _. I give unto _ e _ ~ w _ a _ n _ s _ t _ a _ t _ e _ m _ y _ e ♥ _ u _ b _ e; _ n _ m _ g _ a _ e _ s _ u _ f _ c _ e _ t for all men that ♥ h _ m _ l _ ☼ t _ e _ s _ l _ e _ ♪ b _ f _ r _ ♠ m _; for if they ♥ _ u _ b _ e ☼ _ h _ m _ e _ v _ s ♪ _ e _ o _ e ♠ _ e, _ n _ h _ v _ f _ i _ h _ n ♠ _ e, then will I make w _ a _ t _ i _ g _ b _ c _ m _ s _ r _ n _ ● u _ t _ ♦ t _ e _.

a a a a a b b b c c d d e e e e e e e e e e e e e e e e f f g h

h h h h h h i i i i k k k l l l m m m m m m m m m n n n n

o o o o o r r r s s s s s s s s t t t t t t t t u u u v y y

BLESSINGS ARE YOURS

[HIDDEN MESSAGE]

Cross off the letters J, K, Q, X, and Z to find the scripture. Check page 175 for the reference.

ANDJWHATKISQITZTHATQYEXSHALLJHOPEKFOR?KBEHOLDZIQSAYZ

UNTOQJKYOUZTHATJYEKSHALLQHAVEJHOPEXTHROUGHKTHEXATONE

MENTJOFXCHRISTKANDJTHEQPOWERJOFXHISQRESURRECTION,KTOXB

EQRAISEDJUNTOKLIFEXETERNAL,QANDKTHISZBECAUSEJOFQYOURJFAIT

HKINJHIMXACCORDINGQTOKTHEZPROMISE.

BUILD ON THE ROCK

[MATCHING]

Fill in the blanks of the scripture with the phrases listed. Check page 175 for the reference.

the Son of God	to drag you down
foundation	remember, remember
in the whirlwind	upon which ye are built
his mighty winds	shall beat upon you
and endless wo	of our Redeemer
they cannot fall	your foundation

And now, my sons, ___________, _____________ that it is upon the rock ___ _____ ______________, who is Christ, ___ ___ __ ________, that ye must build _____ _______________; that when the devil shall send forth _____ __________ ________, yea, his shafts ___ ___ ____________, yea, when all his hail and his mighty storm _____ _____ _____ _____, it shall have no power over you ___ _____ _____ ______ to the gulf of misery ____ __________ ____, because of the rock _____ ________ ___ _____ ______, which is a sure __________, a foundation whereon if men build _____ __________ _____.

CENTERED ON THE SAVIOR

[CODE]

Each letter in the passage has been changed to a symbol. For example, G = ¶. Crack the code to find the scripture principle. Check page 176 for the reference and a hint.

§ Ω Θ ↓ ~ → ~ ↓ Ω Θ Ÿ Λ √ * $ % Ω.

CHOOSE THE RIGHT

[CODE]

Each letter in the passage has been changed to a symbol. For example, A=%. Crack the code to find the scripture. Check page 176 for the reference and a hint.

→, √ $ @ $ @ ~ $ √, @ ¢ ¶ → V, % V Θ + $ % √ V

Ÿ # ¶ Θ → @ # V • § ¢ ¢ → X • §; ¢ $ %, + $ % √ V

V • § ¢ ¢ → X • § • → £ $ $ ↓ • § $

^ → @ @ % V Θ @ $ V • ¶ → Ω * → Θ.

DOUBT NOT, FEAR NOT

[CROSSWORD]

Use the clues given to find answers to the crossword. Check page 176 for the reference and a hint.

Across

2. Member of the Godhead (2 words)
4. He who suffered for our sins (2 words)
7. Immoveable, not rattled
9. Not proud, meek
10. Attention and care in the Lord's service
11. One with a personal knowledge of the gospel
12. To accept the truth, have faith in

Down

1. Petitions to Heavenly Father
2. To look forward to the promises of Christ
3. Assured reliance in the Lord
5. The act of being honest and moral
6. Information gained from education
8. Forbearance, wait without complaint

HE WILL BLESS YOU

[CODE]

Some words in the passage have been changed to mathematical equations. Solve the equations and match the words with the numbers. Check page 176 for the reference and a hint.

And now, my (3x5) brethren, I perceive that ye (2x6) still in your (4x5); and it (5x6) me that I must speak (2x8) this thing. For if ye would hearken unto the (3x7) which (5x5) a (3x9) to (2x5), ye would know that ye must (1x10); for the evil (3x7) (5x5) not a (3x9) to (2x5), but (5x5) him that he must not (1x10). But behold, I say unto you that ye must (2x5) always, and not (8x3); that ye must not (5x7) any thing unto the Lord save in the first place ye shall (2x5) unto the Father in the name of Christ, that he will (4x8) thy (6x6) unto thee, that thy (3x12) may be for the (3x6) of thy soul.

HIS TRANSGRESSION

[SCRIPTURE FIND]

Find the missing words of each scripture. Write the found word from each scripture above the corresponding number in the final passage to reveal the theme. Check page 176 for the reference and a hint.

1. Blessed be the name of God, for because of my transgression my eyes (9) _____ opened, (7) ____ in this life I shall have (14) ____, and again in the flesh I shall see God. (Moses 5:10)

2. And in that day the Holy Ghost (2) ____ upon (1) _____, which beareth record of the Father and the Son, saying: I am the Only Begotten of the Father from the beginning, henceforth and forever, that as thou hast fallen thou mayest (6) ____ redeemed, and all mankind, even as many as will. (Moses 5:9)

3. And he cometh into the world (10) _____ he may save all (8) ____ if they will hearken unto his voice; for behold, he suffereth the pains of all (4) ____, yea, the pains of every living creature, both men, women, and children, who belong to the family of Adam. (2 Nephi 9:21)

4. Therefore, (11) _____ have drunk out of the cup of the wrath of God, which justice could no more deny unto them than it could deny (3) _____ Adam should fall because of his partaking of the forbidden fruit; therefore, mercy could (13) _____ claim on them no more forever. (Mosiah 3:26)

5. And he suffereth this that the resurrection (12) _____ pass upon all men, that all (5) _____ stand before him at the great and judgment day. (2 Nephi 9:22)

________ ________ ________ ________ ________
1. 2. 3. 4. 5.

______; ________ ________ ________, ________ ________
6. 7. 8. 9. 10. 11.

________ ________ ________.
12. 13. 14.

LIKE OUR FATHER

[HIDDEN MESSAGE]

Beginning at the shaded square, draw a zigzag line from the top row to the bottom row. Do the same thing starting below the shaded square to complete the scripture. Complete the top section first and then move to the bottom. Check page 176 for the reference.

T	H	E	U	E	D	O	E	E	E	W	F	U	C	D	E	H	E	T		E
S	H	O	R	L	F	B	R	P	I	R	O	E	L	T	T	V	A	N	Y	

A	I	I,	H	R	A	O	E	R	I	A	P	H	R	R	E	H	T.	I
S	S	N	O	E	Y	V	U	N	F	S	T	E	E	F	W	C	O	

LINE UPON LINE

[HIDDEN MESSAGE]

Beginning at the top left square, draw a zigzag line from the top row to the bottom row. Do the same thing starting below the shaded square to complete the scripture. Use the highlighted letters to find the final theme. Check page 176 for the reference.

L	E	A	T	N	E	N	O	H	M	Y	N	U	M	H	N	O	S.
E	E	P	R	H	I	C	T	M	Y	A	O	D	T	E	T	T	K

Unscramble all the highlighted spaces to reveal who Alma counseled to prepare for leadership responsibilities.

_ _ _ _ _ _ _

LULL THEM AWAY

[LETTER CLUE]

Fill in the answer to each clue. Write the numbered letters from the answers above the corresponding numbers in the final scripture principle. If a word is repeated, it is marked with a symbol. Check page 176 for the reference and a hint.

1. The reconciliation with God for mankind through Jesus Christ

   _ _ _ _ _ _ _ _ _
   23 _ 42 11 _ 9 _ 30 4

2. The pure love of Christ _ _ _ _ _ _ _
   43 21 2 _ _ 17 7

3. What brought sin and death into the world

   _ _ _ _   _ _   _ _ _ _
   22 28 37 15   _ _   10 5 31 _

4. Mother, father, and children _ _ _ _ _ _
   34 19 _ 46 24 12

5. God's communication with man _ _ _ _ _ _ _ _ _ _
   _ 48 27 18 16 6 44 _ 35 _

6. Disdain, conceit _ _ _ _ _
   _ 45 29 41 26

7. Sinful, the act of wrongdoing _ _ _ _ _ _ _ _ _ _
   13 _ 20 _ _ 33 47 _ 49 3

8. Godliness, pure _ _ _ _ _ _ _ _
   40 36 1 _ 32 _ 8 39

9. The Holy Ghost is a personage of _ _ _ _ _ _
   25 _ 14 _ 38 _

In the _ _ _ _   _ _ _ _,   _ _ _ _   _ _ _ _
1 2 3 4   5 6 7 8   9 10 11 12   13 14 15 16

_ _ _ _ _   _ _ _ _ _,   _ _ _ _,   _ _ _
17 18 19 20 21   22 23 24 25 26   27 28 29 30   31 32 33

_ _ _ _ _ _ _   _ _ _ _ _ _ _ _ _.
34 35 36 37 38 39 40   41 42 43 44 45 46 47 48 49

OBEDIENCE BRINGS JOY

[HIDDEN MESSAGE]

Starting at the marked word, follow the directions to choose the words on the table. Write the words in the spaces to reveal a scripture with a great blessing. Some words may be used more than once. Check page 177 for the reference.

it	from	unto	spoken	be	suppose	to
Behold	★Do	never	ye	happiness	was	been
that	you	has		concerning	I	restored
because	restoration	sin	wickedness	not	shall	say

Begin★ ____________

Down 2, Right 3____________

Up 3, Right 1 ____________,

Down 3, Left 5 ____________

Up 3 ____________

Down 2, Right 2 ____________

Up 1, Right 4 ____________

Left 3, Up 1 ____________

Right 1, Down 2 ____________

Down 1, Left 3____________,

Up 1, Left 1 ____________

Up 1, Right 3 ____________

Down 2, Right 2 ____________

Up 3, Left 1____________

Down 2, Right 2____________

Up 2, Left 5____________

Down 3, Right 1 ____________

Right 4, Up 3____________

Down 1, Left 2____________.

Left 4____________,

Right 5, Down 1 ____________

Down 1, Right 1 ____________

Up 3, Left 4 ____________

Left 1, Down 2 ____________,

Down 1, Right 2 ____________

Up 2, Left 1____________

Right 3____________

Left 1____________.

PLAIN WORDS

[MATCHING]

Match the reference with the key words for each scripture. Write the letter from the right column on the line with the corresponding number to find the final theme. Check page 177 for the reference and a hint.

1. 2 Nephi 28:7–9	Watch and pray always. (i)
2. 2 Nephi 9:28–29	Learning is good if we follow God's counsel. (e)
3. Mosiah 4:30	Watch your thoughts, words, and deeds. (a)
4. Alma 39:9	We cannot justify any sin. (f)
5. Ether 12:27	Adam fell that men might be. (c)
6. 2 Nephi 2:25	Serving others serves God. (h)
7. Mosiah 2:17	Charity suffereth long. (s)
8. Alma 32:21	Go no more after the lust of your eyes. (s)
9. 3 Nephi 18:15, 20–21	Faith is not a perfect knowledge. (r)
10. Moroni 7:45, 47–48	Build your foundation on Christ. (t)
11. Helaman 5:12	Weak things become strong. (t)

_ _ _ _ _ on the words of _ _ _ _ _ _.
(1 2 3 4 5) (6 7 8 9 10 11)

PRESS FORWARD

[SCRIPTURE FIND]

Fill in the missing words of the scripture by finding the correct word in each given hymn or scripture reference. If a word is repeated, it is marked with a symbol. Check page 177 for the reference and a hint.

And now, my (Hymn #337, title) brethren, after ye have gotten into this (1 Nephi 8:20, 3 words) path, I would (Hymn #153, title) if all is done? (Hymn #191, title), I say unto you, (Hymn #233, title); for ye have not (Hymn #116, title) thus far save it were by the word of (Hymn #134, title) with (Jacob 4:6) faith in (Hymn #114, title), relying wholly (D&C 3:20, 3 words) of him who is (Hymn #68, title) to save. Wherefore, ye must (Hymn #81, title, 2 words) with a (2 Nephi 25:24) in Christ, having a perfect (Hymn #42, title) of hope, and a love of (Hymn #68, title) and of all men. Wherefore, if ye shall (Hymn #81, title, 2 words), feasting upon the (Colossians 3:16, 3 words), and (D&C 14:7, 4 words), behold, thus saith the (Hymn #133, title): Ye shall have (D&C 5:22, 2 words).

SINCERE PRAYER

[WORD SCRAMBLE]

Unscramble the words listed below. Place the unscrambled words on the correct lines in the passage to reveal the scripture. If a word is repeated, it is marked with a symbol. Check page 177 for the reference.

elar ttnine	eeerivc eesth gtishn
xtreho	stmifnae eth tthru
repwo	fi eesth gtishn rea ont rteu
eeisnrc rhaet	iftha
ey lwodu ska	ey yam okwn het tthur

And when ye shall ________ ____ ________, I would ________ you that ____ ________ ________ God, the Eternal Father, in the name of Christ, ____ _______ _______ _______ ________ ________; and if ye shall ask with a ________ ________, with ________ ________, having _______ in Christ, he will _________ ______ _______ of it unto you, by the ♥ _______ of the Holy Ghost. And by the ♥ _________ of the Holy Ghost _______ ______ _______ ______ _________ of all things.

SURE FOUNDATION

[LETTER DROP]

Discover the following scripture principle by dropping the letters at the top into the correct boxes directly below them. Read the scripture left to right. Some words have been done for you. The highlighted spaces all contain the same letter. Check page 177 for the reference and a hint.

O	C N W	H I L L	I R T T Y	E H I V	~~B~~ E M S S	P S T T ~~Y~~	A T	A B ~~E~~ N ~~O~~	A ~~A~~ D ~~N~~ T	I ~~N~~ S	I J O S	A E N N ~~W~~	~~E~~ G S S T	A U	N O S	U S	R
				■	B	Y	■			▒				■			
■	■					▒	■	O	N	■			▒		▒	■	■
■					▒		■	C	A	N	■	W	E	■	■	■	■
■					▒					■	▒				'	▒	■
■	■	■											▒ .	■	■	■	■

THE COMFORTER TESTIFIES

[MATCHING]

Match the reference with the key words for each scripture. Write the letter from the right column on the line with the corresponding number to find the final theme. Check page 177 for the reference and a hint.

1. 2 Nephi 32: 8–9	The natural man is God's enemy. (u)
2. Alma 41:10	By grace we are saved. (l)
3. Moroni 7:41	Ye must pray always. (r)
4. Alma 37:35	Learn in thy youth to keep the commandments. (e)
5. 3 Nephi 12:48	Jesus Christ overcame sin and death. (t)
6. 2 Nephi 25:23	I will go and do. (r)
7. Ether 12:6	Witness comes after the trial of faith. (s)
8. Alma 7:11–13	We are free to choose. (h)
9. 1 Nephi 3:7	Ye should be perfect. (a)
10. Mosiah 3:19	Endure to the end. (t)
11. 2 Nephi 31:19–20	Have hope through the Atonement of Christ. (v)
12. 2 Nephi 2:27	Wickedness never was happiness. (e)

The Holy Ghost _ _ _ _ _ _ _   _ _ _ _ _.
1 2 3 4 5 6 7   8 9 10 11 12

THE GREATEST OF ALL

[WORD SEARCH]

Search forward, backward, up, down, and diagonally to find the words and phrases missing from the scripture below. Unscramble the intersecting letters to form the word that belongs in the highlighted spaces. Check page 177 for the reference and a hint.

N	S	O	N	S	A	P	O	S	S	E	S	S	E	D
S	F	H	T	E	I	V	N	E	J	A	Y	E	D	S
Z	U	O	B	E	L	I	E	V	E	T	H	N	B	M
H	D	F	R	Y	Q	I	N	I	Q	U	I	T	Y	V
O	R	W	F	E	Y	L	L	Z	B	K	M	G	V	F
A	C	J	C	E	V	M	W	E	L	L	R	T	E	D
H	E	A	R	T	R	E	G	I	G	E	D	P	E	R
S	F	T	P	X	I	E	R	H	N	A	O	I	E	H
E	P	I	H	P	S	B	T	E	C	H	F	T	V	T
E	H	X	L	E	E	U	E	H	N	I	S	P	O	E
K	O	S	P	L	R	A	D	A	R	I	E	R	L	R
E	P	U	E	T	E	N	R	U	R	W	Q	A	E	U
T	E	F	O	E	H	D	P	H	I	E	J	Y	R	D
H	T	R	E	J	O	I	C	E	T	H	T	C	U	N
T	H	I	N	K	E	T	H	T	B	K	R	H	P	E

And ________ ________ long, and is ____, and _______ not, and is not puffed up, ________ not her own, is not easily provoked, ________ no evil, and ________ not in ________ but rejoiceth in the ________, ________ all things, ____________ all things, ________ all things, ________ all things. . . . But ________ is the _____ ______ of ________, and it endureth ________; and whoso is found ____________ of it at the last day, it shall be ________ with him. Wherefore, my beloved brethren, ______ unto the Father with all the ________ of ________, that ye may be ________ with this love, which he hath bestowed upon all who are true followers of his Son, Jesus Christ; that ye may become the ______ of God; that when he shall ________ we shall be like him, for we shall ___ him as he is; that we may have this ____; that we may be ________ even as he is pure. Amen.

THE LORD'S HANDS

[WORD SEARCH]

Search forward, backward, up, down, and diagonally to find words and phrases that apply to Mosiah 2:17. Unscramble the intersecting letters to find two ways we can be the Lord's hands. Check page 177 for a hint.

E	Q	A	R	I	R	K	E	C	L	O	N	R	A	E	L
B	C	D	F	M	H	S	G	P	K	Z	H	H	I	N	A
A	S	O	H	E	I	K	H	T	H	G	I	M	Z	L	B
U	D	S	M	A	F	N	D	O	J	N	R	I	E	D	O
S	N	A	R	M	G	L	D	I	F	I	T	E	Z	Y	R
D	F	P	H	S	A	M	H	U	D	K	Y	E	C	T	O
F	G	O	R	X	H	N	S	T	R	E	N	G	T	H	P
J	F	I	S	O	J	N	D	Y	H	X	C	F	H	A	F
L	R	U	E	C	F	B	G	M	S	R	L	S	F	N	T
W	J	E	R	V	K	I	F	R	E	C	N	K	V	K	E
I	K	Y	V	B	L	V	T	P	G	N	B	G	T	S	A
S	L	N	I	E	P	C	S	A	Q	B	T	L	G	H	C
D	C	E	C	N	R	O	F	X	B	N	V	S	B	W	H
O	B	R	E	M	R	O	E	H	A	L	C	H	H	F	K
M	N	W	J	P	O	A	F	B	C	R	E	A	T	E	D

_ _ _ _ and _ _ _ _

THE PRECEPTS OF MEN

[MATCHING]

Fill in the blanks of the scripture with the phrases listed. Check page 177 for the reference.

well with us

saved in the kingdom of God

their counsels from the Lord

with a few stripes

for tomorrow we die

for tomorrow we die

shall be in the dark

nevertheless, fear God

committing a little sin

because of his words

for thy neighbor

and foolish doctrines

Yea, and there shall be many which shall say: Eat, drink, and be merry, ____ ___________ ____ ____; and it shall be _____ ______ ___. And there shall also be many which shall say: Eat, drink, and be merry; __________, _____ _____—he will justify in __________ __ _____ ____; yea, lie a little, take the advantage of one _______ __ ___ _______, dig a pit ____ ____ _____________; there is no harm in this; and do all these things, ____ _____________ ___ ____; and if it so be that we are guilty, God will beat us ____ __ ____ _______, and at last we shall be _______ __ ___ __________ __ ___. Yea, and there shall be many which shall teach after this manner, false and vain ____ __________ ___________, and shall be puffed up in their hearts, and shall seek deep to hide ______ _________ _____ ___ _____; and their works _____ __ __ ___ ______.

THESE THINGS WE DO

[WORD SEARCH]

Search forward, backward, up, down, and diagonally to find words and phrases that apply to 2 Nephi 25:23–26. Check page 178 for a hint.

A	B	E	L	I	E	V	E	M	A	L	N
P	D	O	B	X	F	G	T	H	J	E	T
R	V	Q	R	E	K	E	I	C	F	A	C
E	E	M	A	Q	C	U	R	Y	L	B	X
A	L	C	H	U	D	I	W	K	N	H	P
C	K	Y	O	F	M	A	O	E	A	P	E
H	R	G	S	N	J	B	C	J	K	D	R
E	O	M	G	K	C	S	F	Q	E	L	S
A	B	E	O	F	H	I	O	T	B	R	U
G	A	O	W	A	E	D	L	G	M	E	A
F	L	B	P	R	O	P	H	E	S	Y	D
K	D	N	S	L	M	C	P	N	D	C	E
W	X	R	G	B	H	E	L	G	O	A	X
L	H	O	E	C	A	R	G	V	N	D	B

THEY SPEAK FOR HIM

[CODE]

Each letter in the passage has been changed to a different letter. For example, A has been changed to J (j = a). Crack the code to find the scripture principle. Check page 178 for the reference and a hint.

Jqvmxz zumje io cdm uhkmb hn cdm Dhxo Vdhzc; kdmbmnhbm, cdmo zumje cdm khbgz hn Ldbazc. Kdmbmnhbm, A zjag fqch ohf, nmjzc fuhq cdm khbgz hn Ldbazc; nhb imdhxg, cdm khbgz hn Ldbazc kaxx cmxx ohf jxx cdaqvz kdjc om zdhfxg gh.

TO SAVE OUR SOULS

[CROSSWORD]

Use the clues given inside the passage to find the answers to the crossword and complete the scripture. Some words may be repeated. Check page 178 for the reference and a hint.

And he shall go (onward, 1↓), suffering (hurts, 2↓) and (illnesses, 7↓) and (enticements, 4↓) of (all types, 2 words, 13→); and this that the (basic part of a sentence, 11↓) might be fulfilled which saith he will take upon him the pains and the (diseases, 6↓) of his (persons, 19→). And he will take upon him (passing away, 10↓), that he may (to release the ties, 3 words, 3→) of death which (secure, 8↓) his people; and he will take upon him their infirmities, that his bowels may be filled with (compassion, 20→), according to the (skin, 14→), that he may know according to the flesh how to (give relief, 5↓) his people according to their infirmities. Now the (still small voice, 17→) knoweth all things; nevertheless the (title of Jesus Christ, 3 words, 9→) suffereth according to the flesh that he might take upon him the (wrongdoings, 15→)of his people, that he might blot out their (sins, 18→) according to the power of his (act of saving, 12↓); and now behold, this is the (declaration of truth, 16↓) which is in me.

TO THE END

[WORD SCRAMBLE]

Unscramble the words listed below. Place the unscrambled words on the correct lines in the passage to reveal the scripture. If a word is repeated, it is marked with a symbol. Check page 178 for the reference.

ned	ctawh	nuncitoe
amn	sriphe	vesuyrosel
nigmoc	sutoghht	brmermee
srdow	seded	vebores
dommnatnsemc	tihfa	rahed
negircnocn	vesli	

But this much I can tell you, that if ye do not _ _ _ _ _   _ _ _ _ _ _ _ _ _ _, and your _ _ _ _ _ _ _ _, and your _ _ _ _ _, and your _ _ _ _ _, and _ _ _ _ _ _ _ the _ _ _ _ _ _ _ _ _ _ _ _ of God, and _ _ _ _ _ _ _ _ in the _ _ _ _ _ of what ye have _ _ _ _ _   _ _ _ _ _ _ _ _ _ _ the _ _ _ _ _ _ of our Lord, even unto the _ _ _ of your _ _ _ _ _, ye must ♥ _ _ _ _ _ _. And now, O _ _ _, _ _ _ _ _ _ _ _, and ♥ _ _ _ _ _ _ not.

TRUE WISDOM

[WORD SEARCH]

Search forward, backward, up, down, and diagonally to find the words and phrases missing from the scripture below. If a word is repeated, it is marked with a symbol. Check page 178 for the reference.

H	O	D	S	E	I	T	L	I	A	R	F	U	K	E	J
U	F	W	I	H	L	F	U	S	L	E	A	R	N	E	D
F	D	O	L	A	W	E	S	Z	H	O	L	T	G	N	V
B	D	K	O	T	D	E	X	E	F	E	M	C	Y	H	P
O	G	C	W	L	N	E	B	W	S	N	D	P	F	R	T
H	F	D	E	N	I	K	G	N	A	H	G	J	O	F	C
T	E	R	I	D	O	S	U	P	L	N	E	F	V	J	G
C	I	A	H	S	F	O	H	C	I	Q	I	D	L	G	L
O	V	G	R	E	C	U	D	N	R	T	K	N	P	B	T
D	H	C	O	K	W	I	N	P	E	Y	C	F	E	S	H
V	E	D	B	F	E	U	Y	T	H	S	R	A	R	K	I
C	M	K	J	H	C	N	H	O	B	E	S	S	I	J	N
B	F	O	X	A	N	D	N	C	I	P	M	C	S	I	K
G	S	I	D	P	E	E	N	O	L	I	V	E	H	W	D
Z	A	E	Y	S	T	H	V	F	S	G	S	D	U	C	R
D	M	N	I	D	I	L	C	B	J	A	G	O	D	I	E
C	O	W	K	R	G	W	S	N	E	M	U	T	F	D	O
P	D	O	F	B	M	E	H	N	Z	C	M	K	I	E	A
E	J	C	G	G	N	I	S	O	P	P	U	S	D	V	G
B	F	M	E	I	O	B	J	L	Q	H	A	G	W	K	D

O that __________ plan of the ______ _____! O the __________, and the __________, and the ● __________ of ____! When they are ☼ __________ they ______ they are _____, and they ♪ __________ not unto the ♠ __________ of ♥ _____ for they set it ______, __________ they know of themselves, wherefore, their __________ is ● __________ and it __________ them not. And they shall ________. But to be ☼ __________ is _____ if they ♪__________ unto the ♠ __________s of ♥ _____.

TURN FROM IT

[CROSSWORD]

Use the clues given to find answers to the crossword. Place the answers on the corresponding spaces in the scripture. Some words may be repeated. Check page 178 for the reference.

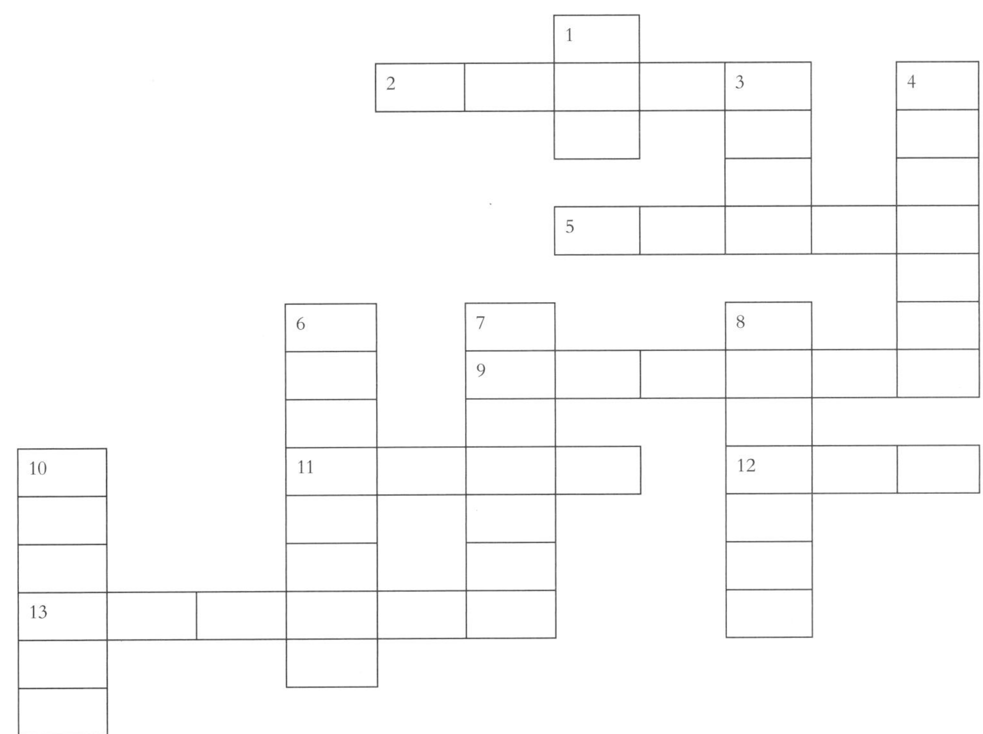

Across

2. The intersection of two lines
5. Strong, unrighteous desires for something
9. Not at all
11. What you see with
12. To whom we pray
13. Not including, everything but

Down

1. Male offspring
3. Acts of wrongdoing
4. To give up entirely
6. To bring back to your mind
7. Getting something from your ancestors
8. Where God reigns
10. To change, turn from sin

Now my [1↓] _____, I would that ye should [10↓] _______ and [4↓] _________ your [3↓] ______, and go no more after the [5→] ________ of your [11→] ________, but [2→] _________ yourself in all these things; for [13→] _________ ye do this ye can in [9→] _________ [7↓] __________ the [8↓] __________ of [12→] _____. Oh, [6↓] ______________, and take it upon you, and [2→] _______ yourself in these things.

UNSEEN TRUTH

[HIDDEN MESSAGE]

Solve the word puzzles in the passage below to complete the scripture. Some words may be repeated. Check page 178 for the reference.

And now, I, (Mother - ther + road - ad + knit - kt), would (sparrow - arrow + beak - b) somewhat (concert - t + canning - can) these (rhymes with sings); I would show unto the (word - d + land - an) that (face - ce + smith - sm) is things which are (home - me + moped - mo) for and not seen; wherefore, (distance - tance + pluto - lo + e) not because ye see not, for ye receive no (with - h + nest - t + s) until after the (trivial - iv) of your faith.

WATCH AND PRAY ALWAYS

[LETTER DROP]

Discover the following scripture by dropping the letters at the top into the correct boxes directly below them. Read the scripture left to right. Some words have been done for you. The highlighted spaces all contain the same letter. Check page 178 for the reference.

Verily, verily, I say unto you, ye must watch and pray always, lest ye be tempted by the devil, and ye be led away captive by him.

B	~~A~~	E	~~D~~	E	A	H	A	~~I~~	G	A	C	A	A	A	E	B	E
F	A	G	H	H	A	H	~~I~~	~~N~~	N	E	E	E	E	H	H	E	E
	B	H	H	H	C	L	~~I~~	N	R	~~M~~	H	H	G	L	M	E	E
	E	~~N~~	I	I	D	L	I	~~T~~	~~S~~	O	O	I	I	O	T	Y	
		T	L	I	E	N	L	T	S	S	R	K	L	R	U	Y	
		W	O	L	E	V	L	U		T	S	V	N	T			
			S	V	R						T		Y	T			
			S		W						~~Y~~			V			
■	A	N	D	■											■		
■	■	■						■	■				■				■
						■	I	N	■	M	Y	■				,	■
■	■						■	I	S	■					,	■	■
■										■					■		
■	■	■						■							,	■	■
						■	I	T	■						■		
■	■						■					■			.	■	■

F	A	A	A	E	A	B	A	E	~~A~~	A	~~D~~	~~A~~	O	~~I~~	B	E	E	~~Y~~
	F	C	H	I	E	D	E	E	A	~~N~~	E	D	O	O	~~N~~	H	~~M~~	
		N	H	I	L	E	L	H	~~N~~	S	~~M~~	O	U	U	R	R		
		T	M	I	L	I	R	~~I~~	N	T	N	S	~~Y~~	R	T			
			P	M	R	Y	S	L	S	U	Y	T	Y		U			
			W	R	V		T	S	W		Y	Y						
■	■	■					■	I	N	■					■	■	■	■
■									■					■				■
					,	■							■	I	N	■	M	Y
■	■				,	■					■						■	■
■	■	■						■	A	N	D						■	■
■	■									■	M	A	Y	■			■	■
■	■	■	■	■	■							.	■	■	■	■	■	■

WE DO BELIEVE

[HIDDEN MESSAGE]

Solve the word puzzles in the passage below to complete the scripture. Some words may be repeated. Check page 178 for the reference.

For we labor (dog - og + ill - l + i + gentleman - eman + y) to write, to persuade our (chick - ck + lid - i + rent - t), and also our (breath - a + rent - t), to (belly - ly + five – fv + have - ha) in Christ, and to be (direct – dit + once – e + filed – f) to God; for we know that it is by (grape - pe + ce) that we are (slave - l + d), after all we can do.

And we (rhymes with walk) of Christ, we (read - ad + join - n + cape - ap) in Christ, we (opposite of post + ache - e) of Christ, we prophesy of Christ, and we (wrist - st + skate - ska) according to our prophecies, that our children may (knife - ife + bow - b) to what (opposite of sweet + cape - ap) they may look for a (read - ad + rhymes with kiss + vision - vis) of their sins.

YIELD TO THE HOLY GHOST

[CROSSWORD]

Use the clues below to determine the words that apply to the scripture found in Mosiah 3:19. Answers are in order from top to bottom. The highlighted area spells the name of an antagonist of our Father in Heaven. Check page 178 for a hint.

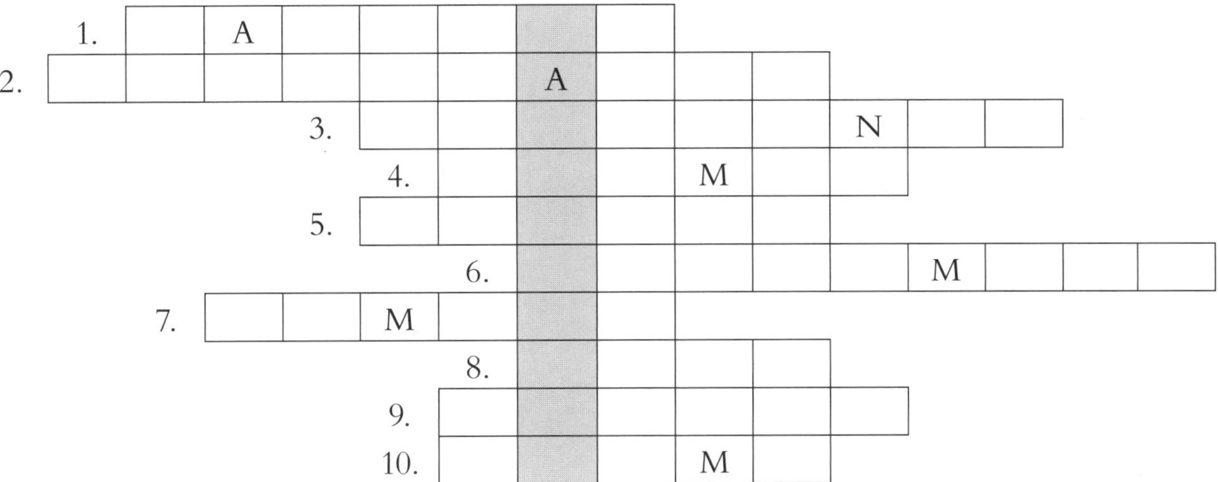

1. To bear pain or trials without complaint
2. Event that introduced spiritual and physical death (3 words)
3. Allurements or temptations
4. Yield or surrender
5. The Savior of the world
6. The sacrifice of our Savior
7. Not prideful
8. Showing patience and longsuffering
9. Those called to enter into a covenant with our Savior
10. One who is against another

DOCTRINE AND COVENANTS PUZZLERS

A PRINCIPLE WITH PROMISE

[WORD SCRAMBLE]

Choose the words and phrases that apply to the Word of Wisdom and that are found in Doctrine and Covenants 89. Cross out the words and phrases *not* found in the section. Unscramble the remaining letters on the spaces below to reveal an important principle. Check page 179 for a hint.

n. all grain

e. flesh . . . of beasts and . . . fowls

a. all meat . . . sometimes

e. adapted to the capacity of the weak

d. hot drinks (are not for the body)

e. tobacco (is not for the body)

h. monosodium glutamate

s. sugar and all sweeteners

b. strong drinks (are not for the belly)

f. carrots and other vegetables

c. fruit of the vine

m. milk, cheese and eggs

r. nuts from below and above the ground

l. honey for sweetening

o. wheat for man

t. hot chocolate

i. all wholesome herbs

__ __ __ __ __ __ __ __ __

A PROMISE

[CODE]

Each letter in the passage has been changed to a different letter. For example, I has been changed to Q (q = i). Crack the code to find the scripture principle. Check page 179 for the reference and a hint.

Q, gxl Wcik, fs ncoak zxla jl kc zxfg Q efj; nog zxla jl kc acg zxfg Q efj, jl xfdl ac hicsqel.

ALL SAINTS

[MATCHING]

Fill in the blanks of the scripture with the phrases listed. Check page 179 for the reference.

wisdom	and not faint
shall pass by them	a promise
in their navel	of knowledge
treasures	and do these sayings
to their bones	obedience to the commandments
and not be weary	of Israel

And all saints who remember to keep ________________________, walking in ________________________, shall receive health __________________ and marrow __________________; And shall find ____________________ and great treasures __________________, even hidden ________________; And shall run ____________________, and shall walk ______________________. And I, the Lord, give unto them ______________, that the destroying angel ____________________, as the children __________________, and not slay them. Amen

APPEARANCES

[MATCHING]

Match the reference with the key words for each scripture. Write the letter from the right column on the line with the corresponding number to find the final theme. Check page 179 for the reference and a hint.

1. D&C 13:1	Look unto Christ in every thought. (s)
2. D&C 46:33	Great joy comes from bringing souls unto Jesus Christ. (V)
3. D&C 130:22–23	The Melchizedek Priesthood administers in spiritual things. (t)
4. D&C 6:36	The Lord is bound to bless the obedient. (i)
5. D&C 107:8	The Aaronic Priesthood was restored. (F)
6. D&C 18:15–16	Jesus Christ was crucified and bore our sins. (o)
7. D&C 82:10	Practice virtue and holiness continually. (i)
8. D&C 1:37–38	Blessings of the Word of Wisdom. (i)
9. D&C 89:18–21	The principles of righteousness give power to the priesthood. (n)
10. D&C 76:40–41	Jesus Christ's words shall all be fulfilled. (s)
11. D&C 121:36, 41–42	The Father and Son have bodies of flesh and bones. (r)

The _ _ _ _ _ (1 2 3 4 5)   _ _ _ _ _ _ (6 7 8 9 10 11)

CELESTIAL GLORY

[SCRIPTURE FIND]

Find the missing words of each scripture. Write the found word from each scripture above the corresponding number in the final passage to reveal the theme. Check page 179 for the reference and a hint.

1. And there he preached to them the (22) _________ gospel, the doctrine of the resurrection and (16) _____ redemption of mankind from (19) _____ fall, and from individual sins on conditions of repentance. (D&C 138:19)
2. These are they whose bodies are celestial, whose glory is that (24) ___ the sun, even the glory of God, the (7) _________ of all, whose glory the sun of the firmament is written of as being typical. (D&C 76:70)
3. But blessed are they who have kept the (23) ________ and observed (6) ____ commandment, for they shall (5) ______ mercy. (D&C 54:6)
4. (1) ______ thus being called by (13) ______ holy calling, and ordained unto the high (17) _________ of the holy order of God, (4) ___ teach his commandments unto the children of men, that they also might (11) ______ into his rest. (Alma 13:6)
5. And a white stone is given to each of those who come (12) _____ the celestial kingdom, whereon is a (20) _____ name written, which no (9) _____ knoweth save he that receiveth it. (D&C 130:11)
6. And see that all these things are done in wisdom and (3) ______; for it is not requisite that (8) __ man should run faster than he has strength. And again, it is expedient that he should be diligent, that thereby he might win the prize; therefore, all things (10) _____ be done in (14) _____. (Mosiah 4:27)
7. Wherefore, (18) _________ the church, thou shalt give heed unto all his words (21) ____ commandments which he shall give unto you as he receiveth them, walking (2) ____ all holiness before me. (D&C 21:4)
8. And they were married, and given in (25) _________, and were blessed according to the multitude (15) ___ the promises which the Lord had made unto them. (4 Nephi 1:11)

_____ (1) ___ (2) _____ (3) ___ (4) ______ (5) ____ (6) ________ (7), __ (8) _____ (9) _____ (10) _____ (11)

____ (12) _____ (13) ______ (14) ___ (15) _____ (16) _________ (17) [_________ (18) ____ (19) ____ (20)

____ (21) _________ (22) _________ (23) ___ (24) _________ (25)].

COME FOLLOW ME

[HIDDEN MESSAGE]

Beginning at the shaded square, draw a zigzag line from the top row to the bottom row. Do the same thing starting below the shaded square to complete the scripture. Complete the top section first and then move to the bottom. Check page 179 for the reference.

L	O	A	D	N	W	F	L	E,	I	N	T	L	E	S	E	E	K	T	E	M	S
W	E	R	R	S;	O	A	M	K	A	N	D	H	I	M	T	E	N	N	O	S	Y

O	A	M	L	S	A	I	E	I	E	A	C	D	I	O	M	S
H	F	L	Y	H	P	V	R	P	T,	A	N	E	Y	N	U	E.

DO GOOD

[LETTER CLUE]

Fill in the answer to each clue. Write the numbered letters from the answers above the corresponding numbers in the final scripture. If a word is repeated, it is marked with a symbol. Check page 179 for the reference and a hint.

1. A model to follow _ _ _ _ _ _ _
   19 12 1 45 51
2. Parents' female child _ _ _ _ _ _ _ _
   25 7 23 5 40 46
3. Responsible for what we do _ _ _ _ _ _ _ _ _ _ _
   10 27 53 50 31 17 2
4. The third member of the Godhead _ _ _ _   _ _ _ _ _
   49 14 8 18 26 52 33
5. The Bible, Book of Mormon, and Doctrine and Covenants _ _ _ _ _ _ _ _ _ _
   4 39 13 32 24 57
6. Marvelous, astonishing _ _ _ _ _ _ _ _ _
   42 6 20 29 56 38 15
7. Acknowledge, make known _ _ _ _ _ _ _
   30 35 3 34 58
8. To rule or reign _ _ _ _ _ _
   48 28 41 55
9. Changed to a glorified state _ _ _ _ _ _ _ _ _ _ _ _
   22 11 54 43 21 9
10. Uncultivated and uninhabited area _ _ _ _ _ _ _ _ _ _
    36 47 44 37 16

Verily I say, _ _ _   _ _ _ _ _ _ be _ _ _ _ _ _ _ _ _
1 2 3 4 5 6 7 8 9 10 11 12 13 14 15 16 17 18

_ _ _ _ _ _ _ in a _ _ _ _   _ _ _ _ _, and do many things of their
19 20 21 22 23 24 25 26 27 28 29 30 31 32 33 34

_ _ _   _ _ _ _   _ _ _ _, and bring to pass
35 36 37 38 39 40 41 42 43 44 45

much _ _ _ _ _ _ _ _ _ _ _ _ _.
46 47 48 49 50 51 52 53 54 55 56 57 58

FINDING JOY IN STRENGTH

[WORD SCRAMBLE]

Unscramble the words listed below. Place the unscrambled words on the correct lines in the passage to reveal the scripture. If a word is repeated, it is marked with a symbol. Check page 179 for the reference and a hint.

peesl rngloe	ledi
deb relay	tulfa
rweya	aclunen
rsiae rleya	sidobe
sinmd	dienrgvitao

Cease to be __ __ __ __; cease to be __ __ c __ __ __ __; cease to find __ __ u __ __ one with another; cease to __ __ __ __ __   __ __ n __ __ __ than is needful; retire to thy __ __ __   __ __ r __ __, that ye may not be __ __ a __ __; __ __ __ __ __   __ __ __ __ __, that your __ __ __ __ __ __ and your __ __ n __ __ may be __ __ v __ __ __ __ __ __ __ __.

FOR ALL

[SCRIPTURE FIND]

Find the missing words of each scripture. Write the found word from each scripture above the corresponding number in the final passage to reveal the theme. Some numbers have been repeated. Check page 179 for the reference and a hint.

1. Yea, even at the last day, when (5) ____ men shall stand to be judged of him, then shall they confess that he is God; then shall they confess, who live without God in the world, that the judgment of an everlasting punishment is just upon them; and they shall quake, and (13) _____, and (22) _____ beneath the glance of his all-searching eye. (Mosiah 27:31)
2. And lo, he shall (8) _____ temptations, and pain of (17) _____, hunger, thirst, and fatigue, even more than man can suffer, except it be unto death; for behold, blood cometh from every (16) _____, so great shall be his anguish for the wickedness and the abominations of his people. (Mosiah 3:7)
3. And it came to pass that when he said (3) _____ words, he commanded his disciples that they should take of the wine of the (21) _____ and (19) _____ of it, and that they should also give unto the multitude that they might drink of it. (3 Nephi 18:8)
4. For, behold, the Lord your Redeemer (2) _____ death in the flesh; wherefore he suffered the (14) ____ of all men, that all men might (9) _____ and come unto him. (D&C 18:11)
5. And now I do know of (11) _____ that they are true; for the Lord (1) _____ hath made them manifest unto me by his Holy Spirit; and this is the (18) _____ of revelation which is in me. (Alma 5:46)
6. And in doing these (4) _____ thou wilt do the (12) _____ good unto thy fellow beings, and wilt promote the glory of him who is your Lord. (D&C 81:4)
7. And it must needs be that the devil should tempt the children of men, or they could (7) _____ be agents unto themselves; for if they never should have (20) _____ they could not know the sweet. (D&C 29:39)
8. And he shall go forth, (10) _____ pains and afflictions and temptations of (15) _____ kind; and this that the word (6) _____ be fulfilled which saith he will take upon him the pains and the sicknesses of his people. (Alma 7:11)

For behold, I, (1) _____, have (2) ________ (3) ______ (4) _______ for (5) ____, that they (6) ______ (7) ____ (8) ________ if they would (9) ________; But if they would (7) ____ (9) _______ they must (8) ________ even as I; Which (10) ___________ caused (11) ________, even (1) _______, the (12) ___________ of all, to (13) __________ because of (14) ______, and to bleed at (15) _____ (16) _____, and to (8) _________ both (17) ______ and (18) _____—and would that I (6) ______ (7) ____ (19) ______ the (20) ______ (21) _____, and (22) __________.

FORGIVE ONE ANOTHER

[LETTER DROP]

Discover the following scripture by dropping the letters at the top into the correct boxes directly below them. Read the scripture left to right. One word has been done for you. The highlighted spaces all contain the same letter. Check page 179 for the reference and a hint.

~~A~~	A	A	A	C	A	D	B	E	D	E	E	A	D	D
H	E	A	C	G	D	R	D	E	E	G	E	E	N	O
M	E	~~D~~	D	I	E	R	D	E	G	H	G	E	N	
S	J	R	E	N	E		E	H	N	H	T	O	T	
	~~N~~	T	H	T	N		L	I	T	R		T	O	
		U	R	W	O		O	O	T	S				
		Y		Y	S		T	U	T	W				
				Y			Y		U					
A	N	D												
						—								
										,				
										.				

FULL HEART

[CROSSWORD]

Use the clues given to find phrases found in the hymnbook. Check page 180 for the reference and a hint.

Across

2. "We'll _______ him by day and by night."
5. "Fill us with ________ we pray."
7. "Swell our hearts with fond emotion, and our joy in thee ________."
8. "This is our hymn of _______ praise."

Down

1. "And praise and _______ give to him who bled on Calvary's hill."
3. "_______, the Lord is King!"
4. "We gather together to ask the Lord's __________."
6. "Will linger in our ____________ hearts."

GIFTS OF THE SPIRIT

[CODE]

Each letter in the passage has been changed to a symbol. For example, N = @. Crack the code to find the scripture principle. Check page 180 for the reference and a hint.

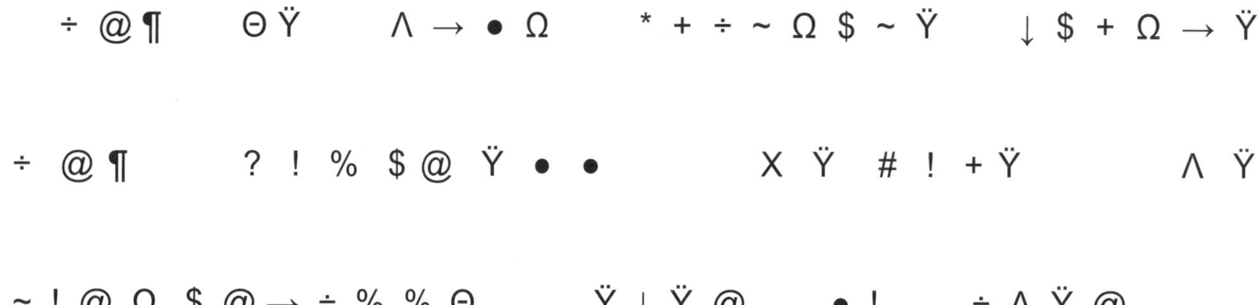

GRATEFUL HEART

[HIDDEN MESSAGE]

Follow the code to find the corresponding words. Write the words on the spaces to discover a scripture with a great blessing. Some words may be used more than once. Fill in the words at the bottom of the puzzle to find the principle of the scripture. Check page 180 for the reference.

	1	2	3	4	5
A	glorious	all	made	unto	he
B	an	more	earth	be	even
C	who	shall	of	yea	with
D	fold	and	receiveth	things	him
E	thankfulness	added	hundred	the	this

Begin

D2 ________ A3 ________ E2________

A5 ________ A1 ________; A4________

C1 ________ D2 ________ D5________,

D3 ________ E4 ________ B5________

A2 ________ D4 ________ B1________

D4 ________ C3 ________ E3________

C5 ________ E5 ________ D1________,

E1 ________ B3 ________ C4________,

C2 ________ C2 ________ B2________.

B4 ________ B4 ________

Receive A2 ________ D4 ________ C5 ________ E1 ________.

HE CAME

[CROSSWORD]

Use the clues given to find answers to the crossword. Place the answers on the corresponding spaces in the scripture. Some words may be repeated. Check page 180 for the reference and a hint.

Across

1. Good news of Jesus Christ
6. A written account
8. To make spotless
9. You use it when you speak or sing
11. The state of being wicked
14. Opposite of went
15. To be nailed to a cross

Down

1. Happy news (2 words)
2. Acts of wrongdoing
3. The Savior of mankind
4. You ___ your testimony
5. Past tense of 4 down
7. Where God dwells (plural)
10. Opposite of in
12. To make clean or holy
13. Earth and all the people on it

And this is the [1→] _______, the [1↓] ____ _________, which the [9→] ________ [10↓] _____ of the [7↓] ________ [5↓] _____ [6→] _______ unto us—That he [14→] _____ into the [13↓] ______, even [3↓] ________, to be [15→] __________ for the [13↓] ________, and to [4↓] _____ the [2↓] ______ of the [13↓] _______, and to [12↓] ________ the [13↓] ________, and to [8→] __________ it from all [11→] ___________________.

HEAR MY VOICE

[HIDDEN MESSAGE]

Cross off the letters Q and K to find the scripture. Check page 180 for the reference.

YEA,QBEHOLD,KIQWILLKTELLQYOUKINQYOURKMINDQANDKINQYOU
RKHEARTQ,BYKTHEQHOLYQGHOSTK,WHICHQSHALLKCOMEQUPONKYOU
QANDKQWHICHQSHALLKDWELLQINKYOURQHEART.

NOWQ,BEHOLDK,THISQISKTHEQSPIRITKOFQREVELATION;KBEHOLD,Q
THISKISQTHEKSPIRITQBYKWHICHQMOSESKBROUGHTQTHEKCHILDREN
QOFKISRAELQTHROUGHKTHEQREDKSEAQONKDRYQGROUNDK.

HEAVENLY COMMUNICATION

[WORD SEARCH]

Search forward, backward, up, down, and diagonally to find words and phrases that apply to Doctrine and Covenants 8:2–3. Check page 180 for a hint.

A	H	L	O	B	L	M	G	E	C	V	M	L	O	T	K	O	P	Y	R
Z	S	G	P	W	R	T	E	Q	R	Y	A	U	I	O	P	L	X	S	B
M	D	T	Z	K	J	R	U	E	S	C	N	B	G	H	J	K	J	V	S
A	V	B	I	D	A	N	V	F	G	H	I	B	N	M	X	Y	T	N	K
K	S	D	M	L	Q	E	K	G	R	I	F	L	A	U	F	Z	G	B	H
E	H	F	C	W	L	L	A	U	D	M	E	Q	I	E	N	I	V	I	D
K	Y	E	R	A	C	S	N	I	E	C	S	F	N	R	S	C	A	K	Q
N	D	B	T	O	U	Z	M	D	G	S	T	H	S	T	H	O	E	G	R
O	G	I	G	L	Y	F	K	A	S	R	Z	T	P	N	S	V	M	Z	A
W	O	K	V	A	L	M	U	N	L	Y	X	D	I	J	R	N	G	W	Y
N	N	W	T	E	X	I	G	C	X	L	P	K	R	U	S	H	O	W	A
C	D	B	P	V	R	A	X	E	H	T	V	M	A	K	L	M	R	F	P
T	R	X	K	E	M	L	J	T	A	Y	Q	O	T	C	V	D	S	I	E
J	E	L	A	R	P	C	G	H	C	N	X	L	I	Z	J	H	B	K	C
D	A	Y	I	J	S	O	Y	E	V	H	N	L	O	C	A	X	P	T	N
E	M	R	C	S	E	R	H	M	D	F	K	B	N	T	E	Z	N	O	D
V	W	H	X	D	F	P	D	L	Z	X	F	S	J	K	Y	J	I	H	L
L	G	S	Y	N	O	C	D	I	S	C	L	O	S	E	R	S	E	R	C
B	Z	O	A	R	B	F	A	U	N	G	W	K	U	P	I	A	G	T	O
U	D	E	P	I	T	S	O	H	G	Y	L	O	H	V	E	X	N	M	W

HIGHER POWER

[HIDDEN MESSAGE]

Starting at the marked word, follow the directions to choose the words on the table. Write the words in the spaces to reveal a scripture with a great blessing. Some words may be used more than once. Complete the final theme using the four unused words. Check page 180 for the reference.

authority	★The	has	of	world	administer	the
Priesthood	the	in	all	spiritual	the	presidency
power	ages	to	Melchizedek	greater	church	priesthood
of	Melchizedek	over	in	offices	and	right
holds	the	all	things	and	the	in

Begin __________

Down 2, Right 2__________

Up 1, Left 3 __________

Down 3__________

Right 5, Up 3__________

Right 1, Down 2__________

Up 3, Left 3__________

Down 1, Right 3__________,

Down 3, Left 2__________

Up 4, Left 2__________

Down 2, Left 2__________

Down 1, Right 5__________

Up 3, Left 5__________

Down 3, Right 2__________

Up 2, Right 1__________

Up 1, Right 3__________

Down 3, Left 2__________

Up 2, Left 2__________

Down 3, Left 1__________

Up 2, Right 4__________

Down 2, Right 1__________

Left 4__________

Up 2, Left 1__________

Down 1, Left 1__________

Right 5, Down 1__________

Up 4, Left 1__________,

Down 2, Left 2__________

Up 2, Right 3__________

Down 3, Left 2 __________

Up 2, Right 1__________

Down 3, Left 1__________.

The __________ is ___ ______ ______.

IN HIS IMAGE

[HIDDEN MESSAGE]

Follow the code to find the corresponding words. Write the words on the spaces to discover a scripture with a great blessing. Some words may be used more than once. Check page 180 for the reference.

	1	2	3	4	5	6	7
A	man	Spirit	the	it	upon	Holy Ghost	Were
B	personage	us	with	a	not	also	dwell
C	tangible	him	receive	Father	man's	body	so
D	tarry	could	as	may	has	is	Son
E	of	flesh	but	bones	in	descend	and

Begin

A3______ A3______ E4______, D2______ D4______

C4______ D7______ E3______ B5______ E6______

D5______ B6______; D6______ B7______ A5______

B4______ E3______ B4______ E5______ C2______

C6______ A3______ B1______ B2______. E7______

E1______ A6______ E1______ B4______ B5______

E2______ D5______ A2______. A1______ D1______

E7______ B5______ A7______ D4______ B3______

E4______ B4______ A4______ C3______ C2______.

D3______ C6______ B5______ A3______

C1______ E1______ C7______, A6______

D3______ E2______ A3______ E7______

C5______; E7______ A6______ A4______

IN THE LIGHT

[WORD SEARCH]

Search forward, backward, up, down, and diagonally to find the words and phrases missing from the scripture below. If a word is repeated, it is marked with a symbol. Check page 180 for the reference.

W	N	A	H	O	Z	X	I	P	Y	J	Z	K	Q	L	K
P	O	C	D	A	R	B	D	E	L	E	E	N	K	C	D
D	I	S	E	V	T	F	U	W	D	Y	O	E	F	E	P
A	T	L	G	F	E	A	H	G	I	S	A	G	L	H	E
J	I	K	L	H	L	R	J	B	D	K	B	I	J	L	R
M	S	N	K	A	O	L	S	E	M	O	V	N	M	O	S
B	O	R	P	S	R	B	V	A	Q	E	R	B	T	M	O
Q	P	U	R	S	V	O	Q	W	R	X	A	R	E	S	N
G	P	J	T	B	L	U	F	V	C	Y	U	H	V	T	A
C	O	W	O	E	X	J	Y	L	Z	K	T	W	L	Y	G
A	C	D	B	I	B	C	A	R	I	F	B	C	C	S	E
D	D	M	D	E	N	D	E	F	O	G	D	G	R	E	S
H	R	O	I	P	J	W	K	E	H	Q	H	I	J	N	K
E	L	I	F	M	O	G	N	L	E	N	F	T	G	I	L
H	J	N	G	P	G	O	D	L	I	N	E	S	S	R	I
K	O	Q	L	H	N	P	Q	M	O	K	P	L	Q	T	M
N	P	U	R	O	T	N	S	O	T	P	R	N	O	C	P
Q	D	I	S	T	U	R	B	E	R	U	R	V	S	O	Q
T	U	R	V	W	A	T	S	S	E	N	K	R	A	D	U
W	B	E	A	S	T	R	A	E	H	Y	C	G	Z	J	N

1. finding myself alone, I ______ down

2. began to offer up the desires of my heart to ______.

3. Thick _________ gathered around me,

4. all my powers to call upon God to _________ me

5. I saw a ________ ____ ______ exactly over my head,

6. I saw two ________________, whose brightness and glory

7. "This is My ________ ____. Hear Him!"

8. My object in going to ___________ of the Lord

9. was to know which of all the sects was _______.

10. that I might know which to ______.

11. I was answered that I must join ______ ___ ______,

12. draw near to me with their lips, but their ________ are far from me,

13. they teach for ____________ the commandments of men,

14. having a form of _______________,

15. but they deny the _________ thereof.

16. It seems as though the ______________ was aware,

17. that I was destined to prove a ___________ and an annoyer of his kingdom;

18. Why the ______________ and persecution that arose against me,

JESUS CHRIST LIVES

[WORD SEARCH]

Search forward, backward, up, down, and diagonally to find the words and phrases missing from the scripture below. If a word is repeated, it is marked with a symbol. Check page 181 for the reference.

D	R	O	C	E	R	G	N	I	R	A	E	B	S	E	K
J	F	H	T	B	X	C	D	U	I	L	M	O	C	R	V
S	N	S	E	V	I	L	E	H	T	A	H	T	B	I	L
G	V	E	S	L	F	U	Z	X	E	N	F	G	S	G	X
L	C	O	T	Z	V	N	E	C	I	E	U	A	T	H	N
Z	N	V	I	J	H	C	K	M	L	T	A	I	N	T	M
M	E	Y	M	C	G	S	X	L	U	T	Y	Z	A	H	O
F	X	A	O	M	E	O	A	T	V	O	O	N	T	A	F
B	I	Y	N	B	L	F	H	B	N	G	C	V	I	N	B
V	H	T	I	E	O	R	V	U	Z	E	E	Y	B	D	C
K	O	Z	E	T	O	M	F	J	I	B	A	S	A	I	H
E	A	U	S	U	A	H	D	L	G	Y	B	I	H	L	Z
U	B	A	G	E	U	B	X	U	N	L	D	M	N	M	G
I	L	H	M	G	L	S	K	C	E	N	Y	E	I	J	K
N	C	Y	S	D	L	R	O	W	X	O	Z	V	O	H	X
S	O	N	S	A	N	D	D	A	U	G	H	T	E	R	S

And now, after the many ____________ which have been given of _________, this is the testimony, _____ _____ _____, which we give of him: _____ _____ _____! For we saw him, even on the ______ ______ of God; and we heard the [1 word] ________ [2 words] ______ _______ that he is the ______ _______ of the Father—That by him, and _________ him, and of him, the ______ are and were created, and the ____________ thereof are begotten _______ ___ ________ unto God.

JOY AND COMFORT

[CODE]

Each letter in the passage has been changed to a different letter. For example, E has been changed to X (x = e). Crack the code to find the scripture principle. Check page 181 for the reference and a hint.

Rkxhxcqhx, wocb ls bkt kxghb gza hxfqonx, gza nwxgex lzbq bkx nqexzgzbd rkonk bkql kgdb igax.

KEYS TO BAPTIZE

[HIDDEN MESSAGE]

Cross off the letters B, F, and G to find the scripture. Check page 181 for the reference.

T	B	H	E	G	B	A	A	B	R
O	N	F	I	C	F	P	F	F	R
G	I	E	G	S	G	T	G	H	O
O	D	G	W	A	B	S	B	R	E
S	G	T	G	O	R	F	E	G	D

LISTEN

[CODE]

Each letter in the passage has been changed to a mathematical equation. For example, A = 5. Solve the equations to match the letters with the numbers. Check page 181 for the reference and a hint.

3x5 5+5 2+3 8x8 8+8 3x9 3+3 6x6 6+5 5+5

_ _ _ _ _ _ _ _ _ _

2x7 2+3 6x5 2+5 3x9 8x8 2+3 8+8 4+4

_ _ _ _ _ _ _ _ _

3x5 2+5 2x7 6x6 2x5 2x8 6x6 3x9

_ _ _ _ _ _ _ _

5+6 2+5 2x7 5x5 3x9 8x8 2x4 2x7

_ _ _ _ _ _ _ _

OBEY THE LAW

[SCRIPTURE FIND]

Find the missing words of each scripture. Write the found word from each scripture above the corresponding number in the final passage to reveal the theme. Check page 181 for the reference and a hint.

1. There (10) ____ a law, irrevocably decreed in heaven before the foundations of this world, (16) ______ which all blessings are (20) ______________. (D&C 130:20)
2. For all who will have a blessing at my hands shall abide the (15) _____ (17) _______ was appointed for that blessing, and the conditions thereof, as were instituted (7) ______ before the foundation of the world. (D&C 132:5)
3. (1) ____ it is my will that you shall humble yourselves before me, and (4) ______ this (6) ________ by your diligence and humility and the prayer of faith. (D&C 104:79)
4. And my people must needs be chastened until they learn (12) ___________, if (18) ____ must needs be, (11) ____ the things which they suffer. (D&C 105:6)
5. Behold, all these are kingdoms, and any man who hath seen (5) ____ or the least of these hath seen (8) _______ moving in his majesty and power. (D&C 88:47)
6. Whether (9) _____ be good, or whether it be evil, we will obey the voice of the Lord our God, (13) ____ whom we send thee; that it may be well with us, (2) ______ we obey the voice of the Lord our God. (Jeremiah 42:6)
7. And (3) ____ are his witnesses of these things; and so (19) ____ also the Holy Ghost, whom God hath given to them (14) ______ obey him. (Acts 5:32)

____ ______ ____ _______ ____ _________ _____ _____,
1 2 3 4 5 6 7 8

__ __ __ _________ __ _____ ____ ____ ______ __ __
9 10 11 12 13 14 15 16 17 18 19

_____________.
20

(D&C 130:21)

OUR LIKENESS

[HIDDEN MESSAGE]

Solve the word puzzles to complete the passage below. Some words may be repeated. Check page 181 for the reference.

mother - mor __________

Faith - i + er __________

hand - h __________

South - uth + n __________

shave - s __________

bo + ladies - la __________

opposite of on - f __________

fl + chess - chs + h __________

random - rom __________

boot - ot + nest - t __________.

SCRIPTURE PUZZLERS

POWER AND INFLUENCE

[CROSSWORD]

Use the clues given to find answers in the crossword. Check page 181 for the reference and a hint.

Across

1. Deceit, cunning
3. Not having; lacking
7. Clean, virtuous
9. Authority of God given to men
11. Poor in spirit, teachable
13. Patient for an extended time (2 words)
14. Benevolence

Down

1. Kind and quiet, not harsh or violent
2. Affection, charity
4. Talk one way and act another
5. Gently causing people to believe or do something, influential
6. Intelligence, education gives
8. To give greater scope, make bigger
10. Not hypocritical or fake
12. Body and spirit together

POWER TO BLESS

[CODE]

Each letter in the passage has been changed to the letter that follows it in the alphabet. Crack the code to find the scripture principle. Check page 181 for the reference and a hint.

S g d L d k b g h y d c d j O q h d r s g n n c h r s g d f q d z s d q o q h d r s g n n c z m c z c l h m h r s d q r h m r o h q h s t z k s g h m f r.

POWERFUL PRINCIPLES

[LETTER DROP]

Discover the following scripture by dropping the letters at the top into the correct boxes directly below them. Read the scripture left to right. Some words have been done for you. The highlighted spaces all contain the same letter. Check page 181 for the reference and a hint.

H	A	~~A~~	A	E	E	D	C	A	E	A	D	A	B	~~A~~	E	D
H	A	A	D	E	E	E	C	A	E	D	G	E	~~H~~	B	H	F
O	E	C	E	E	E	H	E	C	E	D	L	E	H	F	O	N
~~T~~	F	C	H	G	H	I	E	E	I	E	N	H	I	F	O	
T	~~H~~	E	H	H	I	N	N	L	I	E	O	~~T~~	N	L	O	
	H	E	I	L	N	N	O	O	L	I	R	T	O	O	R	
	H	N	O	N	N	P	O	O	N	L	S	T	O	O	~~T~~	
		R	O	N	R	P	O	R	N	N	S	W	S	P	Y	
		R	~~T~~	P	T	R	P	T	N	P	S		S	S		
		T	T	V	T	T	S	W	P	R	Y		T	S		
		T	V					W	R	R			U	T		
									U	S						
T	H	A	T	■			▒	■							■	■
		■			▒	■				▒						
■			▒	■				▒								■
■	■					▒			▒		■					■
■	■			▒	■				▒			■			■	■
■		▒			▒	,	■				■	T	H	A	T	■
■	■			▒	■				▒			■			■	■
	▒			▒		■							■		▒	■
■	■									▒		■				■
					▒		■					■				
		▒	■									▒		■		
■	■						▒					▒		.	■	■

PREACH UNTO THE WORLD

[CROSSWORD]

Use the clues given to find answers to the crossword. Check page 181 for the reference and a hint.

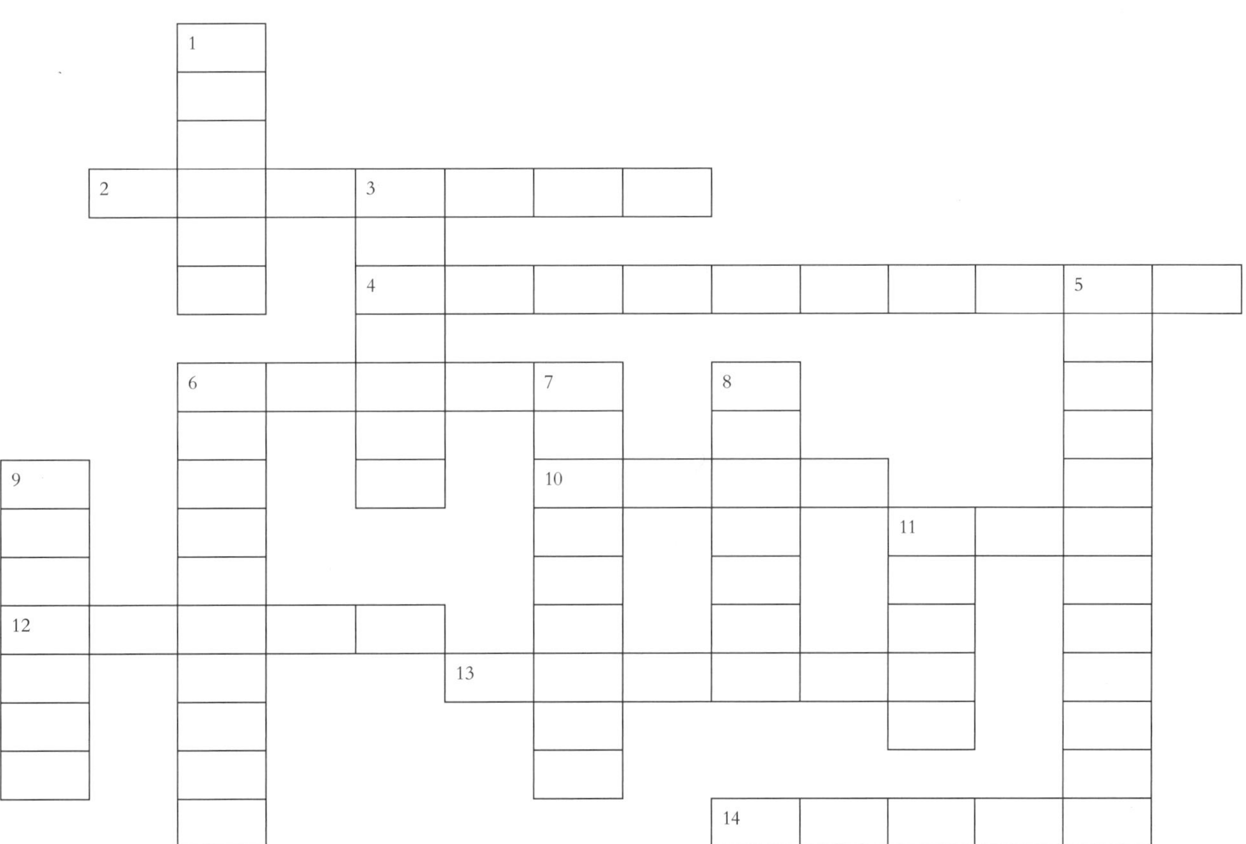

Across

2. The work of the Lord on earth
4. The act of seeking forgiveness
6. Hope for things that are true
10. Title of Christ
11. Male child
12. To instruct
13. The good news of Jesus Christ
14. Son of Joseph and Mary

Down

1. The Lord and Savior of mankind
3. Help to benefit others
5. Written on stone tablets; decrees
6. The underlying support; basic doctrine
7. Third member of the Godhead (two words)
8. Showing praise and love for God
9. The first ordinance of the gospel
11. Spirits and bodies united

PRIESTHOOD POWER

[MATCHING]

Fill in the blanks of the scripture with the phrases listed. Write the corresponding letter in the blanks on the right to complete the phrase below that spells a characterisitc of this blessing. Check page 181 for the reference.

repentance (o)	servants (a)
from the earth (i)	of the ministering of angels (h)
in righteousness (y)	Priesthood of Aaron (t)
Messiah (u)	do offer again an offering (t)
immersion for the remission of sins (r)	

Upon you my fellow ________________, ___

in the name of ________________ ___

I confer the __________ ___ ________, ___

which holds the keys __ ____ __________ __ ________, ___

and of the gospel of ________________, ___

and of baptism by ________ ___ ___ __________ ___ ____; ___

and this shall never be taken again _____ ___ _________, ___

until the sons of Levi __ _____ ______ ___ _________ ___

unto the Lord __ ______________. ___

The Priesthood of Aaron is the __________________ to baptize.

SAVE OUR WORLD FROM SIN

[WORD SEARCH]

Search forward, backward, up, down, and diagonally to find words and phrases that apply to Doctrine and Covenants 76:40–41. Unscramble the intersecting letters to find the final theme. Check page 181 for a hint.

H	B	E	T	A	T	F	S	A	S	O	N	O	F	G	O	D	X
F	S	O	K	B	G	T	E	S	T	I	M	O	N	Y	O	R	R
Y	V	D	R	I	H	T	V	T	P	B	J	G	K	O	S	H	D
F	E	M	E	L	G	P	W	R	E	C	F	L	L	R	J	G	E
I	R	G	D	E	I	F	I	C	U	R	C	B	C	F	F	K	T
T	U	H	B	E	L	D	C	R	O	Y	N	C	F	E	D	L	C
C	A	K	C	M	E	T	D	G	R	T	P	A	S	H	S	H	E
N	X	M	N	V	E	R	N	A	R	W	O	S	L	K	A	V	R
A	R	L	A	E	C	R	V	E	U	B	I	M	S	L	I	E	R
S	M	S	A	I	R	L	H	H	M	D	R	V	A	G	I	R	U
L	P	W	H	B	A	T	A	A	Y	E	E	N	R	O	M	F	S
B	O	E	F	C	A	S	L	K	E	F	N	O	D	C	N	Y	E
U	W	R	E	F	J	O	S	L	R	J	F	O	E	A	B	U	R
D	E	T	G	W	H	V	M	A	P	G	I	R	T	N	C	R	C
C	R	O	S	S	Y	K	D	O	E	Q	N	T	N	A	W	O	D

The _ _ _ _ _ _ _ _ _

SEARCH THE SCRIPTURES

[SCRIPTURE FIND]

Fill in the missing words of the scripture by finding the correct word in each given hymn or scripture reference. If a word is repeated, it is marked with a symbol. Check page 182 for the reference and a hint.

Search these commandments, for they are (rhymes with blue) and (face - ce + with - w + opposite of empty - l), and the (opposite of con + phones - ons + cities - it) and (prod - d + miss - s + es) which are in them shall all be fulfilled.

What I the Lord have (s + poke + no - o), I have spoken, and I excuse not (another word for me); and though the (heat - t + v + hen - h + s) and the (rhymes with birth) pass away, my (rhymes with something that flies in the sky) shall not pass away, but shall all be (opposite of empty – l + f + billed – b), whether by mine own (v + choice - ch) or by the voice of my (serve - e + small insects), it is the same.

THE BITTER CUP

[LETTER CLUE]

Fill in the answer to each clue. Write the numbered letters from the answers above the corresponding numbers in the final scripture. Check page 182 for the reference and a hint.

1. Experiencing pain or loss _ _ _ _ _ _ _ _ _
27 45 10 54 41 59

2. The great act to overcome the consequences of sin _ _ _ _ _ _ _ _ _
17 3 25 31 56 12

3. The act of turning from sin and seeking forgiveness _ _ _ _ _ _ _ _ _ _
15 7 36 43 19 39 46 29

4. To shake slightly from fear _ _ _ _ _ _ _
40 4 58 6 52 55

5. Offered something most precious _ _ _ _ _ _ _ _ _ _
37 49 18 26 35 30

6. That which gives our bodies life _ _ _ _ _ _
44 16 34 24 8

7. The gift received baptism _ _ _ _ _ _ _ _ _
50 21 2 32 1 28 48

8. The faithful shall inherit _ _ _ _ _ _ _ _ _ _ _ _ _
22 53 20 57 9 42

9. A call upon God _ _ _ _ _ _
33 11 5 14 38

10. First principle of the gospel _ _ _ _ _
23 51 47 13

Nevertheless, _ _ _ _ _ _ _ _ _ the _ _ _ _ _ _, and I
1 2 3 4 5 6 7 8 9 10 11 12 13 14 15

_ _ _ _ _ _ _ and _
16 17 18 19 20 21 22 23 24 25 26 27 28 29 30 31 32 33 34 35 36 37 38 39 40 41 42 43 44

_ _ _ _ the _ _ _ _ _ _ _ _ of _ _ _.
45 46 47 48 49 50 51 52 53 54 55 56 57 58 59

THY WILL BE DONE

[CODE]

Each letter in the passage has been changed to a symbol. For example, A = !. Crack the code to find the scripture principle. Check page 182 for the reference and a hint.

% $ → @ →   Ÿ ? ~ X → ¶ ’ →   • ↓ ~ Λ →   → ? ! # #

! # #   > $ * @ # * X # # $ Λ.

TO OVERCOME

[SCRIPTURE FIND]

Choose the correct bolded word for the following scriptures. Write the chosen word from each scripture above the corresponding number in the final passage to reveal the theme. Check page 182 for the reference.

1. And [**stand** or **pray**] for thy brethren of the Twelve. (D&C 112:12)
2. For men ought [**often** or **always**] to pray and not to faint. (D&C 101:81)
3. And prepare for the revelation which is to [**come** or **be**], when the veil of the covering of my temple, in my tabernacle, which hideth the earth, shall be taken [**over** or **off**], and all flesh shall see me together. (D&C 101:23)
4. For we have a labor to perform whilst in this tabernacle of clay, that we may [**defeat** or **conquer**] the enemy of all righteousness, and rest our souls in the kingdom of God. (Moroni 9:6)
5. And in that day [**Satan** or **the devil**] shall not have power to tempt any man. (D&C 101:28)
6. Inasmuch as ye are cut off for transgression, ye cannot [**escape** or **avoid**] the buffetings of Satan until the day of redemption. (D&C 104:9)
7. These were taught faith in God, repentance from sin, vicarious baptism for the remission of sins, the gift of the Holy Ghost by the laying on of [**blessings** or **hands**]. (D&C 138:33)
8. And the [**people** or **servants**] of God shall go forth, saying with a loud voice: Fear God and give glory to him. (D&C 133:38)
9. And whatsoever nation shall [**uphold** or **support**] such secret combinations, to get power and gain, until they shall spread over the nation, behold, they shall be destroyed. (Ether 8:22)
10. Go thy way and do as I have told you, and fear not thine enemies; for they shall not have power to stop my [**work** or **gospel**]. (D&C 136:17)

_____ (1) _____ (2), that you may _____ (3) _____ (3) conqueror; yea, that you may _____ (4) _____ (5),

and that you may _____ (6) the _____ (7) of the _____ (8) of _____ (5) that do _____ (9) his _____ (10).

WHAT'S IT WORTH?

[MISSING-LETTER WORDS]

Every other letter is missing from the words in this scripture. The letters are listed in alphabetical order below. If a word is repeated, it is marked with a symbol. Check page 182 for the reference.

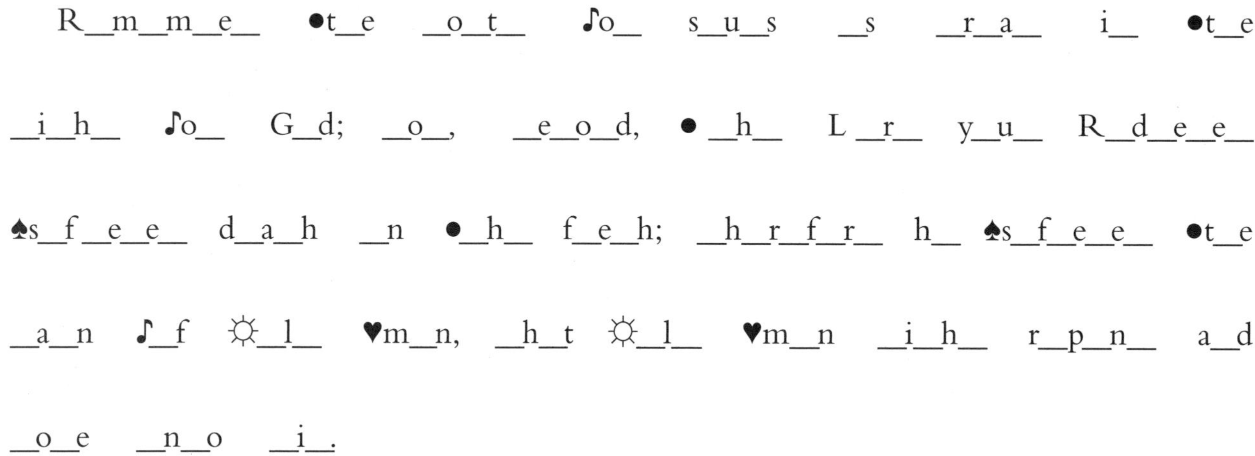

R__m__m__e__ ●t__e __o__t__ ♪o__ s__u__s __s __r__a__ i__ ●t__e

__i__h__ ♪o__ G__d; __o__, __e__o__d, ● __h__ L__r__ y__u__ R__d__e__e__

♠s__f__e__e__ d__a__h __n ●__h__ f__e__h; __h__r__f__r__ h__ ♠s__f__e__e__ ●t__e

__a__n ♪__f ☼__l__ ♥m__n, __h__t ☼__l__ ♥m__n __i__h__ r__p__n__ a__d

__o__e __n__o __i__.

a a a b b c d d d e e e e e e e e e e e e e e e f f f f f

g g g h h h h h h i i i l l l l l m m m m n n o o o o o

o p r r r r r r r s s t t t t t t t t t u u u w w

WHERE DO I LOOK?

[MATCHING]

Match the reference with the key words for each scripture. Write the letter from the right column on the line with the corresponding number to find the final theme. Check page 182 for the reference and a hint.

1. D&C 25:13	Revelation comes to your mind and heart. (s)
2. D&C 58:27	Pray always. (o)
3. D&C 10:5	The worth of souls is great. (u)
4. D&C 76:22–24	Jesus Christ suffered for all of us. (t)
5. D&C 18:10–11	Learn of Christ, listen to his words. (t)
6. D&C 78:19	The first vision. (h)
7. D&C 19:23	We should forgive all men. (i)
8. D&C 58:42–43	Cleave to your covenants. (L)
9. D&C 88:124	Jesus Christ lives. (k)
10. JS—H 1:15–20	Be anxiously engaged in a good cause. (o)
11. D&C 131:1–4	Receive all thing with thankfulness. (n)
12. D&C 64:9–11	Cease to be idle and unclean. (C)
13. D&C 8:2–3	To repent we must confess and forsake sin. (o)
14. D&C 19:16–19	The new and everlasting covenant of marriage. (r)

__ __ __ __   __ __ __ __   __ __ __ __ __ __.

1 2 3 4   5 6 7 8   9 10 11 12 13 14

SCRIPTURE PUZZLERS

WITHOUT FEAR

[LETTER CLUE]

Fill in the answer to each clue. Write the numbered letters from the answers above the corresponding numbers in the final scripture. Check page 182 for the reference and a hint.

1. A name for the Holy Ghost _ _ _ _ _ _ _ _ _ _
   20 38 29 36

2. One tenth _ _ _ _ _ _ _
   18 11 23 37

3. The last book in the New Testament _ _ _ _ _ _ _ _ _ _ _
   16 34 1 35 7 26

4. The stone which is cut out of the _ _ _ _ _ _ _ _ _ _
   3 27 39 6

5. The first ordinance of the gospel _ _ _ _ _ _ _ _
   28 24 9

6. Christ made this possible for all men _ _ _ _ _ _ _ _ _ _ _ _ _ _
   10 21 15 2

7. Repent and seek _ _ _ _ _ _ _ _ _ _ _ _ _
   33 8 22 14 30 13

8. Meekness _ _ _ _ _ _ _ _ _ _
   19 5 32 17

9. Three degrees of glory _ _ _ _ _ _ _ _ _ _
   4 12 25 31

_ _ _ _   _ _ _ _   _ _   _ _   _ _ _ _ _   _ _ _ _ _ _ _;   _ _ _ _ _
1 2 3 4   5 6 7 8   9 10   11 12   13 14 15 16 17   18 19 20 21 22 23 24   25 26 27 28 29

_ _ _,   _ _ _ _   _ _ _.
30 31 32   33 34 35 36   37 38 39

WORK TO SAVE SOULS

[CODE]

Some words in the passage have been changed to mathematical equations. Solve the equations to match the letters with the numbers. Check page 182 for the reference.

And if it so be that you should (4x5) all your days in (3x5) (7x5) unto this people, and bring, save it be one (3x4) unto me, how (12x3) shall be your (8x5) with him in the (2x8) of my (2x12)! And now, if your (10x4) will be (6x6) with one (2x6) that you have brought unto me into the (4x4) of my (3x8), how (12x3) will be your (10x4) if you should bring many (2+10) unto me!

soul or souls = 12	Father = 24
crying = 15	repentance = 35
kingdom = 16	great = 36
labor = 20	joy = 40

YOU ARE FORGIVEN

[HIDDEN MESSAGE]

Follow the code to find the corresponding words. Write the words on the spaces to discover a scripture with a great blessing. Some words may be used more than once. Check page 182 for the reference.

	1	2	3	4	5
A	and	sins	he	the	may
B	of	confess	if	his	repented
C	more	Behold	them	repenteth	will
D	is	a	same	By	this
E	behold	know	Lord	no	the
F	who	remember	of	has	forgiven
G	man	I	forsake	ye	them

Begin

C2_______,

A3_______

F1_______

F4_______

B5_______

B1_______

B4_______

A2_______,

E5_______

D3_______

D1_______

F5_______,

A1_______

G2_______,

A4_______

E3_______,

F2_______

C3_______

E4_______

C1_______.

D4_______

D5_______

G4_______

A5_______

E2_______

B3_______

D2_______

G1_______

C4_______

F3_______

B4_______

A2_______—

E1_______,

A3_______

C5_______

B2_______

G5_______

A1_______

G3_______

C3_______.

REFERENCES AND HINTS FOR PUZZLERS

OLD TESTAMENT

HINTS AND REFERENCES

BECOMING ONE Ezekiel 37:15–17

another
children
companions
Ephraim
hand
house
Israel
join
Joseph
Judah
Lord
one
Son of Man
stick
thine
word
write

BELIEVE AND KNOW Isaiah 29:13–14

Across

1. near
4. wisdom
6. proceed
10. marvellous
11. work
12. people
13. lips
14. heart
16. understanding
17. hid
18. prudent

Down

2. removed
3. wise men
5. fear
7. precept
8. mouth
9. men
11. wonder
13. Lord
15. taught

CHERISHED GIFTS FROM GOD Key words for Psalm 127:3

1. Moses 7:18 — Zion—one heart and one mind in righteousness.
2. Abraham 3:22–23 — Abraham was chosen before he was born.
3. Genesis 2:24 — Husbands and wives should be one.
4. Exodus 19:5–6 — Ye shall be a holy nation.
5. Joshua 24:15 — Choose to serve the Lord.
6. Psalm 24:3-4 — Clean hands and a pure heart.
7. Malachi 4:5–6 — Elijah will turn the hearts of fathers and children.
8. Isaiah 1:18 — Though your sins be as scarlet.
9. Isaiah 29:13–14 — A marvellous work and a wonder.
10. Isaiah 58:3–7 — The law of the fast.

11. Jeremiah 1:4–5 — Jeremiah was foreordained before birth.
12. Amos 3:7 — God reveals His secret to His prophets.

CHOSEN ONES Exodus 19:5–6

children
covenant
earth
holy nation
Israel
kingdom
obey
peculiar
people
priests
speak
treasure
voice
words

CLAIM YOUR BLESSINGS! Application of Psalm 24:3–4

celestial
enter
kingdom
pure
ordinances
repent
temple
worthy

CLEAN THROUGH HIM Isaiah 1:18

COMING PROMISE Application of Malachi 3:8–10

burned
coming
day
people
sacrifice
Son of Man
tithing
tithed
today

COVENANT KEEPERS Joshua 24:15

whom
choose
dwell
evil
gods
fathers
flood
house
land
Lord
other
serve
side

ESTABLISH MY WORDS Application of Ezekiel 37:15–17

The highlighted letter is E.

FEEL HIS PRESENCE NEAR Isaiah 58:6–7

FLEE TEMPTATION Genesis 39:9

The highlighted letter is H.

GUIDING BEACON Psalm 119:105

HONOR THIS DAY Isaiah 58:13–14

Words found more than once:

delight
doing
holy
own
pleasure
sabbath
thee
thine
thy

I WILL, I WILL Psalm 24:3–4

LOOK INSIDE 1 Samuel 16:7

Across
2. look
6. outward
7. height
8. appearance
10. seeth

Down
1. looketh
2. Lord
3. countenance
4. stature
5. man
7. heart
9. refused

MAN OF GRIEF Isaiah 53:5 Full reference: Isaiah 53:3–5

1. Savior
2. Atonement
3. resurrection
4. Jesus Christ
5. spiritual death
6. suffering
7. qualified
8. priesthood
9. body
10. power

MY GLORY Moses 1:39

a = g	b = p	c = t	d = y	e = b	f = n	j = o	l = d	o = m	q = a
r = h	s = k	t = i	u = r	v = w	w = f	x = e	y = s	z = l	

NEVER LED ASTRAY Amos 3:7

a = l	b = g	c = n	d = p	e = a	f = d	g = r	h = t	j = s	k = u
l = w	m = e	n = y	o = i	p = h	q = o	r = b	t = c	x = v	

NO MATTER WHAT Proverbs 3:5–6

1. Genesis 39:9 — Joseph resisted temptation.
2. Moses 1:39 — This is God's work and glory.
3. Isaiah 58:13–14 — The Sabbath is the Lord's holy day.
4. Genesis 1:26–27 — God created man in His own image.
5. Malachi 3:8–10 — Paying tithing brings blessings.
6. 1 Samuel 16:7 — The Lord looks on the heart.
7. Ezekiel 37:15–17 — The Bible and the Book of Mormon are joined together.
8. Psalm 119:105 — God's word is a lamp unto my feet.
9. Isaiah 52:3–5 — Jesus Christ bore our griefs and suffered for our sins.
10. Exodus 20:3–17 — The Ten Commandments.
11. Isaiah 5:20 — Woe unto them that call evil good.

OFFERINGS AND BLESSINGS Malachi 3:9–10 Full reference: Malachi 3:8–10

ON THE SIXTH DAY Genesis 1:26–27

Across
1. creeping
3. cattle
6. male
8. air
9. dominion
12. sea
13. female
14. fish

Down
1. created
2. earth
4. make
5. man
7. likeness
10. over
11. image
14. fowl

PRECIOUS ONES Psalm 127:3

6	9	10	12	14	15	18
are	of	the	children	and	Lo	heritage

20	24	25	27	28	30	45
an	his	Lord	is	womb	fruit	reward

PREMORTAL BEINGS Abraham 3:22–23

Abraham
among
born
chosen
good
great
intelligences
midst
noble
organized
rulers
souls
spirits
world

PRIESTHOOD KEYS RESTORED Malachi 4:5–6

behold
children
coming
curse
dreadful
earth
Elijah
fathers
great
heart
prophet
smite
turn

PURIFIED BY OBEDIENCE Application of Exodus 19:5–6

1. children
2. hope
3. family
4. charity
5. kingdom
6. sacrifice
7. faith
8. peculiar
9. love
10. covenants

RELY ON HIS GUIDANCE Proverbs 3:5–6

1. wisdom
2. thankfulness
3. believe
4. reliance
5. knowledge
6. prayer
7. truth
8. worthy
9. adversity
10. commandments
11. teaching
12. obedient

THE LORD'S ERRAND Key words for Joshua 24:15

c = 10	d = 15	e = 20	h = 25	l = 22
o = 28	r = 30	t = 33	s = 32	v = 35

THE TEN COMMANDMENTS: PART 1 Exodus 20:3–7

bow down
children
commandments
earth
iniquity
jealous
likeness
graven image
guiltless
heaven
name
serve
vain
water
Lord
love
mercy
fathers
God
gods

THE TEN COMMANDMENTS: PART 2 Exodus 20:8–11

cattle
daughter
earth
God
heaven
holy
hallowed
labour
Lord
maidservant
manservant
rested
sabbath
sea
seventh
six
son
stranger
work

THE TEN COMMANDMENTS: PART 3 Exodus 20:12–17

adultery
against
bear
commit
covet
days
false witness
father
God
honour
house
kill
land
long
Lord
maidservant
manservant
mother
neighbour
steal
wife

TOGETHER FOREVER Genesis 2:24

UNITED IN PURPOSE Moses 7:18

A	B	C	D	E	F	G	H	I	L	M	N	O	P	R	S	T	U	W	Y	Z
%	£	*	Θ	$	Ω	v	§	#	+	@	V	→	↓	√	¶	•	X	¥	z	¢

VOICE OF WARNING Application of Amos 3:7

WISE IN THEIR OWN EYES Isaiah 5:20

a = t	b = w	d = u	e = d	f = m	g = v	h = r	i = n	j = o	k = f	l = b
n = p	o = c	q = e	r = i	s = l	t = g	u = k	x = h	y = a	z = s	

WISE PURPOSE Jeremiah 1:4–5

NEW TESTAMENT

HINTS AND REFERENCES

A CITY SET ON A HILL Key words for Matthew 5:14–16

1. 1 Corinthians 15:40–42	The degrees of glory.
2. Matthew 16:19	The keys of the kingdom.
3. 2 Thessalonians 2:1–3	Apostasy foretold.
4. Matthew 28:19–20	Teach and baptize all nations.
5. Revelation 20:12	Judged before God.
6. Hebrews 12:9	God is the Father of our spirits.
7. John 14:15	"If ye love me, keep my commandments."
8. James 2:17–18	Faith without works is dead.
9. Acts 2:36–38	Repent, be baptized, and receive the Holy Ghost.
10. John 3:5	Born of water and of the Spirit.
11. 1 Corinthians 6:19–20	Your body is a temple.
12. Ephesians 4:11–12	Apostles and prophets help perfect the Saints.

A HOUSE OF GOD 1 Corinthians 6:19–20

1. studying
2. chastity
3. knowledge
4. gospel
5. worshipping
6. Book of Mormon
7. obedience
8. honesty
9. authority
10. powerful
11. ordinance

A SACRED GIFT Application of 1 Corinthians 6:19–20

birth
baptism
chastity
choose
clean
health
holy
image of God
modesty
physical
respect
sacred
spirit
temptations
Word of Wisdom
worthy

ALL WILL LIVE AGAIN 1 Corinthians 15:20–21

Matthew 11:28–30	Come unto me.
Matthew 22:36–39	Love the Lord, and love thy neighbor.
Luke 24:36–39	A resurrected body has flesh and bones.
John 14:6	The way, the truth, and the life.
John 17:3	Knowing God and Jesus Christ is eternal life.
Acts 3:19–21	The times of restitution.
Galatians 5:22–23	Fruit of the Spirit.
Philippians 4:13	I can do all things through Christ.
2 Timothy 3:15–17	Scripture given for doctrine, reproof, and correction.
1 Peter 4:6	The gospel is preached to the dead.
James 1:5–6	If you lack wisdom, ask God.

ALWAYS NEAR Application of Philippians 4:13

A	C	D	E	F	G	H	I	J	N	O	Q	R	S	T	U	W
↑	Ÿ	X	~	+	↓	☼	#	%	@	$	&	♈	<	*	♦	♥

ASCENSION FOR ALL 1 Corinthians 15:20–21

Hymn #5, vs. 4, last word
Hymn #218, vs. 2, nineteenth word
Hymn #122, vs. 1, sixteenth word
Hymn # 134, title, last word
Hymn #29, title, fourth word
Hymn #49, vs. 1, first word
Hymn #79, vs. 3, last word

ASK TO KNOW Key words of James 1:5–6

b = a	e = d	f = e	g = f	h = g	i = h	j = i	m = l
n = m	o = n	p = o	t = s	u = t	w = v	x = w	z = y

BE BAPTIZED John 3:5

a = t	b = r	c = k	d = h	e = b	f = p	g = x	h = v	i = u	j = g	l = j	m = i
n = e	o = s	p = l	q = n	r = w	s = d	t = o	v = y	w = m	x = c	y = f	z = a

BE NOT AFRAID Luke 24:36–39

Hymn #141, title, first word
Hymn #108, vs. 3, first four words
Hymn #98, vs. 1, fifteenth word
Philippians 1:28, fourth word
Deuteronomy 7:21, fifth word
Hymn #179, vs. 1, twentieth word
Hymn #277, vs. 3, fourteenth word
Hymn #115, vs. 1, eighteenth word
Hymn #191, vs. 2, tenth word
Hymn #191, vs. 2, twelfth word
Hymn #129, vs. 1, twenty-ninth word
Hymn #175, vs. 2, seventeenth word

BOUNTEOUS BLESSINGS Galatians 5:22–23

faith
fruit
gentleness
goodness
joy
longsuffering
love
meekness
peace
Spirit
temperance

DIVINE GUIDANCE James 1:5–6

Across
1. faith
5. Him
7. wavering
9. wave
10. upbraideth

Down
2. tossed
3. liberally
4. wisdom
6. wind
8. God

EVERLASTING BLESSING John 17:3

FIND REFUGE IN ME Matthew 11:28–30

FOREVER BOUND Matthew 16:15–19

GOOD NEWS FOR ALL 1 Peter 4:6

HEAVENLY KINGDOMS 1 Corinthians 15:40–42

Across
1. celestial
5. terrestrial
9. resurrection
10. raised
12. also
15. corruption
16. moon
18. differeth

Down
2. star
3. another
4. telestial
6. glory
7. dead
8. incorruption
11. stars
13. sun
14. sown
17. one

HELP FROM ON HIGH Philippians 4:13

HOW CAN WE KNOW THE WAY? John 14:6

2	6	8	9	10	11	12	14	15	16	18	25	21	24	30	32	33	45
I	unto	him	and	saith	No	Jesus	am	the	way	man	cometh	truth	Father	but	life	by	me

JUDGMENT DAY Revelation 20:12

a = f	b = a	c = l	d = j	e = d	f = r	g = e	h = p	j = h	m= c	n = o
o = t	q = s	r = m	s = u	t = i	u = k	v = w	x = g	y = b	z = n	

PERFECTED STATE Key words for Luke 24:36–39

PREPARE FOR BLESSINGS Application of Acts 2:36–38

The highlighted letter is T.

RESTITUTION FORETOLD Acts 3:19–21

SHINE ON! Matthew 5:14–16

The highlighted letter is S.

Across
1. bushel
3. candlestick
7. Father
8. light
9. your
10. hid
11. giveth
14. world
15. men
16. glorify

Down
2. heaven
4. shine
5. city
6. candle
11. good
12. house
13. hill
14. works

TEACH AND BAPTIZE Matthew 28:19–20

The highlighted letter is L.

THE GOOD FIGHT James 2:17–18

THE GREATEST TWO Matthew 22:36–39

THE REASON WE OBEY John 14:15

1. Job 36:11
2. Nehemiah 1:11
3. D&C 13:1
4. Daniel 7:27
5. Romans 2:7
6. Hebrews 5:9

THEIR TEACHINGS Application of Ephesians 4:11–14

Abraham
Adam
Daniel
Elijah
Isaiah
Jacob
Jonah
Malachi
Moses
Noah
Samuel

TO PERFECT US Ephesians 4:11–12

The Highlighted letter is S.

WALK IN THE SPIRIT Key words for Galatians 5:22–23

1. meekness
2. charity
3. gentleness
4. longsuffering
5. kindness
6. joy
7. temperance
8. forgiveness
9. faith
10. knowledge
11. love
12. gratitude

WHAT SHALL WE DO? Acts 2:36–38

apostles
assuredly
baptized
Christ
crucified
gift
heard
heart
Holy Ghost
Israel
Jesus
God
Lord
Men
pricked
remission
Repent

WHEN WILL HE COME? 2 Thessalonians 2:1–3

WHOM THE LORD LOVES Hebrews 12:9

WITH ALL THY HEART Application for John 14:15

grace
love
might
mind
perfect
perfected
power
strength
ungodliness

WORDS OF INSPIRATION 2 Timothy 3:15–17

BOOK OF MORMON

HINTS AND REFERENCES

A PARTICLE Alma 32:21

1. suffering
2. exercise
3. forgiveness
4. truth
5. Jesus Christ
6. action
7. Holy Ghost
8. following
9. obedience
10. patient
11. Father
12. keep

AGENCY 2 Nephi 2:27

BE OBEDIENT 1 Nephi 3:7

BE TEACHABLE Mosiah 3:19

natural man
fall of Adam
enticings of the Holy Spirit
atonement of Christ the Lord
submissive
humble
full of love
enemy to God
forever
becometh a saint
becometh as a child
meek
patient
willing to submit

BE WISE Mosiah 2:17

1. labor
2. missionary work
3. volunteer
4. opportunities
5. helping hand
6. charity
7. contributions
8. benevolence
9. forgiveness
10. knowledge

BECOMING STRONG Ether 12:27

BLESSINGS ARE YOURS Moroni 7:41

BUILD ON THE ROCK Helaman 5:12

CENTERED ON THE SAVIOR Keywords for Moroni 7:41

A	C	E	F	G	H	I	M	N	O	P	R	S	T	U	V
§	Λ	~	Ÿ	¶	√	$	→	↓	Θ	+	*	%	Ω	X	¥

CHOOSE THE RIGHT Alma 37:35

A	B	C	D	E	F	G	H	I	K	L	M	N	O	P	R	S	T	U	W	Y
%	~	^	Θ	$	Ω	*	§	#	£	+	@	V	→	↓	√	¶	•	X	Ÿ	¢

DOUBT NOT, FEAR NOT Application of Alma 32:21

Across
2. Moroni 7:32
4. Romans 5:1
7. Enos 1:11
9. Alma 37:33
10. 1 Nephi 15:11
11. D&C 14:8
12. Hebrews 11:6

Down
1. Alma 9:20
2. Jacob 4:6
3. Alma 57:27
5. Galatians 5:5
6. Ephesians 4:13
8. 1 Thessalonians 1:3

HE WILL BLESS YOU 2 Nephi 32:8–9

10	12	15	16	18	20	21
pray	ponder	beloved	concerning	welfare	hearts	spirit
24	25	27	30	32	35	36
faint	teacheth	man	grieveth	consecrate	perform	performance

HIS TRANSGRESSION 2 Nephi 2:25

LIKE OUR FATHER 3 Nephi 12:48

LINE UPON LINE Keywords for Alma 37:35

LULL THEM AWAY Application of 2 Nephi 28:7–9

1. Atonement
2. charity
3. Fall of Adam
4. family
5. revelation
6. pride
7. wickedness
8. holiness
9. spirit

OBEDIENCE BRINGS JOY Alma 41:10

PLAIN WORDS Keywords for 2 Nephi 32:3

PRESS FORWARD 2 Nephi 31:19–20

Hymn #337, title, third word	1 Nephi 8:20, words 6–8
Hymn #153, title, third word	Hymn #191, title, first word
Hymn #233, title, first word	Hymn # 116, title, first word
Hymn #134, title, last word	Jacob 4:6, twenty-ninth word
Hymn #114, title, last word	D&C 3:20, words 32–34
Hymn #68, title, second word	Hymn #81, title, words 1–2
2 Nephi 25:24, seventeenth word	Hymn #42, title, fourth word
Hymn #68, title, last word	Hymn #81, title, words 1–2
Colossians 3:16, words 3–5	D&C 14:7, words 8–11
Hymn #133, title, first word	D&C 5:22, words 25–26

SINCERE PRAYER Moroni 10:4–5

SURE FOUNDATION Application of Helaman 5:12

The highlighted letter is S.

THE COMFORTER TESTIFIES Keywords for Moroni 10:4–5

THE GREATEST OF ALL Moroni 7:45, 47–48

appear	filled	possessed	seeketh	beareth	forever
pray	sons	believeth	heart	pure love	suffereth
Christ	hope	purified	thinketh	endureth	hopeth
rejoiceth	truth	energy	iniquity	see	well
envieth	kind				

THE LORD'S HANDS Application of Mosiah 2:17

created	might	strength	learn
commandments	mind	teach	wisdom
forever	praise	thanks	service
king	prosper	unprofitable	labor

THE PRECEPTS OF MEN 2 Nephi 28:7–9

THESE THINGS WE DO Application of 2 Nephi 25:23, 26

believe	persuade	rejoice	grace	preach	look
talk	labor	prophesy	write	reconciled	

THEY SPEAK FOR HIM 2 Nephi 32:3

j = a	i = b	l = c	g = d	m = e	n = f	v = g	d = h	a = i	e = k
x = l	q = n	h = o	u = p	b = r	z = s	c = t	f = u	k = w	o = y

TO SAVE OUR SOULS Alma 7:11-13

Across
3. loose the bands
9. Son of God
13. every kind
14. flesh
15. sins
17. spirit
18. transgressions
19. people
20. mercy

Down
1. forth
2. pains
4. temptations
5. succor
6. sicknesses
7. afflictions
8. bind
10. death
11. word
12. deliverance
16. testimony

TO THE END Mosiah 4:30

TRUE WISDOM 2 Nephi 9:28–29

TURN FROM IT Alma 39:9

UNSEEN TRUTH Ether 12:6

WATCH AND PRAY ALWAYS 3 Nephi 18:15, 20–21

WE DO BELIEVE 2 Nephi 25:23, 26

YIELD TO THE HOLY GHOST Application of Mosiah 3:19

1. Alma 20:29
2. Mosiah 4:7
3. 2 Nephi 9:39
4. Mosiah 24:15
5. 2 Nephi 10:3
6. 2 Nephi 9:7
7. 1 Nephi 16:5
8. 2 Nephi 27:30
9. Philippines 4:21
10. Mosiah 16:5

DOCTRINE AND COVENANTS

HINTS AND REFERENCES

A PRINCIPLE WITH PROMISE Application of Doctrine and Covenants 89

A PROMISE Doctrine and Covenants 82:10

f = a	n = b	k = d	l = e	x = h	q = i	s = m	a = n	c = o
h = p	i = r	e = s	g = t	o = u	d = v	z = w	j = y	w = l

ALL SAINTS Doctrine and Covenants 89:18–21

APPEARANCES Keywords for Joseph Smith—History 1:15–20

CELESTIAL GLORY Doctrine and Covenants 131:2

Full Reference Doctrine and Covenants 131:1–4

COME FOLLOW ME Doctrine and Covenants 19:23

DO GOOD Doctrine and Covenants 58:27

example, daughter, accountable, Holy Ghost, scriptures
wonderful, confess, govern, transfigured, wilderness

FINDING JOY IN STRENGTH Doctrine and Covenants 88:124

idle, unclean, fault, sleep longer, bed early
weary, arise early, bodies, minds, invigorated

FOR ALL Doctrine and Covenants 19:16–18

Full Reference Doctrine and Covenants 19:16–19

FORGIVE ONE ANOTHER Doctrine and Covenants 64:11

Full Reference Doctrine and Covenants 64:9–11

The highlighted letter is T.

FULL HEART Application for Doctrine and Covenants 78:19

Across
2. "We Thank Thee, O God, for a Prophet," *Hymns* #19
5. "In Fasting We Approach Thee," *Hymns* #139
7. "Lord, Accept Our True Devotion," *Hymns* #107
8. "For the Beauty of the Earth," *Hymns* #92

Down
1. "We'll Sing All Hail to Jesus' Name," *Hymns* #182
3. "Rejoice, the Lord Is King," *Hymns* #66
4. "Prayer of Thanksgiving," *Hymns* #93
6. "As Now We Take the Sacrament," *Hymns* #169

GIFTS OF THE SPIRIT Doctrine and Covenants 46:33

A = ÷	C = ~	E = Ÿ	H = ?	L = %	N = @	P = ★	S = ●	U = →	Y = Θ
B = X	D = ¶	F = #	I = $	M = Λ	O = !	R = +	T = Ω	V = ↓	

GRATEFUL HEART Doctrine and Covenants 78:19

HE CAME Doctrine and Covenants 76:40–41

bear, Jesus, voice, glad tidings, bore, world, cleanse, sins, sanctify, unrighteousness, out, crucified, record, heavens, came, gospel

HEAR MY VOICE Doctrine and Covenants 8:2–3

HEAVENLY COMMUNICATION Doctrine and Covenants 8:2–3

declare, show, proclaim, Holy Ghost, inspiration, divine, still small voice, reveal, revelation, manifest, guidance, disclose, signs, prophecy, make known, dream, vision

HIGHER POWER Doctrine and Covenants 107:8

IN HIS IMAGE Doctrine and Covenants 130:22–23

IN THE LIGHT Joseph Smith—History 1:15–20

kneeled	opposition	pillar of light	none of them	power
disturber	deliver	adversary	personages	right
inquire	Beloved Son	join	God	
doctrines	darkness	hearts	godliness	

JESUS CHRIST LIVES Doctrine and Covenants 76:22–24

JOY AND COMFORT Doctrine and Covenants 25:13

a = d	b = t	c = f	d = s	e = v	f = j	g = a	h = r	i = m	k = h
l = u	n = c	o = i	q = o	r = w	s = p	t = y	w = l	x = e	z = n

KEYS TO BAPTIZE Keywords for Doctrine and Covenants 13:1

LISTEN Keywords for Doctrine and Covenants 19:23

A = 5	D = 8	E = 10	F = 6	H = 11	I = 7	L = 15
N = 16	O = 27	R = 64	S = 14	T = 36	V = 30	W = 25

OBEY THE LAW Application of Doctrine and Covenants 82:10

OUR LIKENESS Doctrine and Covenants 130:22–23

POWER AND INFLUENCE Keywords for Doctrine and Covenants 121:36, 41–42

POWER TO BLESS Keywords for Doctrine and Covenants 107:8

The letter Z will precede the letter A.

POWERFUL PRINCIPLES Doctrine and Covenants 121:36

Full reference Doctrine and Covenants 121:36, 41–42

The highlighted letter is E.

PREACH UNTO THE WORLD Keywords for Doctrine and Covenants 18:10–11

souls	baptize	Jesus	gospel	worship	faith
Holy Ghost	teach	Son	foundation	Lord	mission
service	Christ	repentance	commandments		

PRIESTHOOD POWER Doctrine and Covenants 13:1

SAVE OUR WORLD FROM SIN Application of Doctrine and Covenants 76:40–41

Atonement	Lamb	blood	power	Calvary	third
resurrected	cross	sanctify	crucified	saved	forgive
eternal life	Son of God	Father	testimony		

SEARCH THE SCRIPTURES Doctrine and Covenants 1:37–38

true	faithful	prophecies	promises
spoken	myself	heavens	earth
word	fulfilled	voice	servants

THE BITTER CUP Doctrine and Covenants 19:19

suffering	spirit	Atonement	Holy Ghost	repentance
kingdom of God	tremble	prayer	sacrificed	faith

THY WILL BE DONE Application of Doctrine and Covenants 1:37–38

A = !	B = >	C = Ÿ	D = Λ	E = $	F = ★	H = ?	I = X
J = %	L = #	O = ↓	R = ~	S = →	T = ¶	U = @	W = •

TO OVERCOME Doctrine and Covenants 10:5

WHAT'S IT WORTH? Doctrine and Covenants 18:10–11

WHERE DO I LOOK? Keywords for Doctrine and Covenants 6:36

WITHOUT FEAR Doctrine and Covenants 6:36

Comforter	tithing	Revelation	mountain	baptism
resurrection	forgiveness	humility	kingdoms	

WORK TO SAVE SOULS Doctrine and Covenants 18:15–16

YOU ARE FORGIVEN Doctrine and Covenants 58:42–43

ANSWER KEY FOR PUZZLERS

OLD TESTAMENT

ANSWER KEY

BECOMING ONE

Witnesses

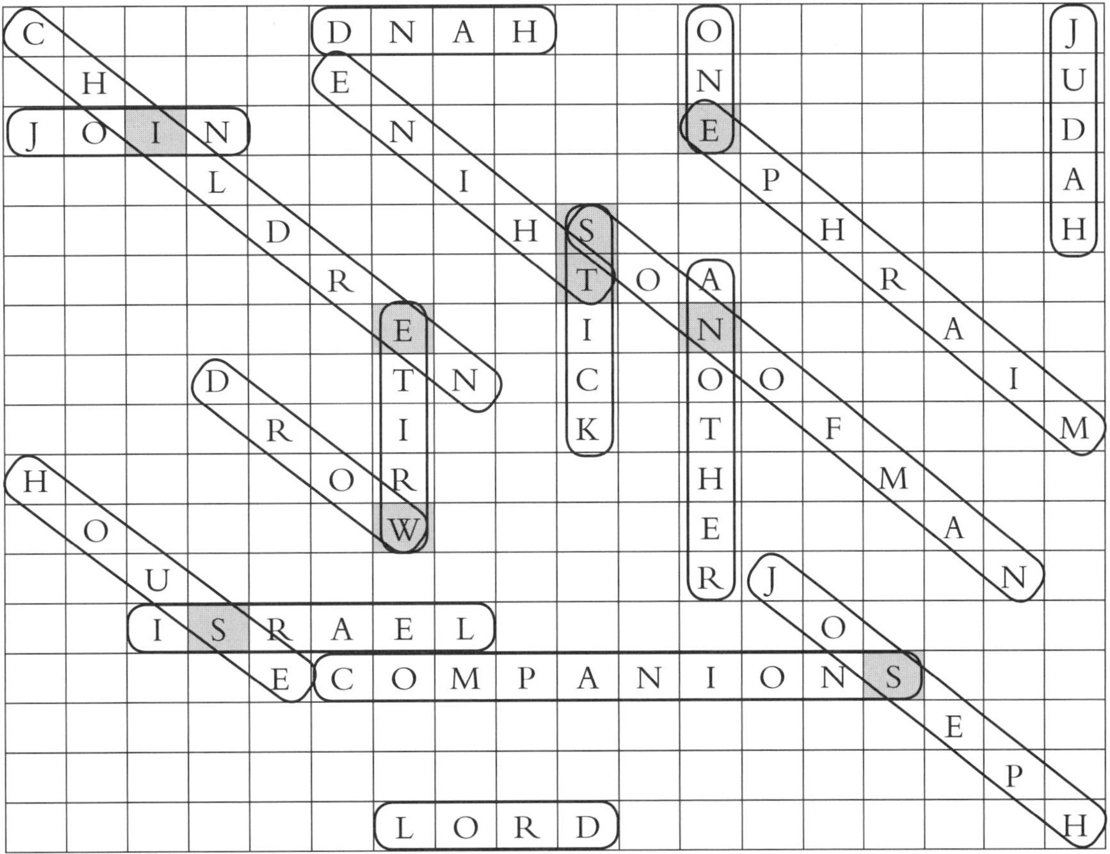

BELIEVE AND KNOW

Wherefore the Lord said, Forasmuch as this people draw near me with their mouth, and with their lips do honour me, but have removed their heart far from me, and their fear toward me is taught by the precept of men: Therefore, behold, I will proceed to do a marvellous work among this people, even a marvellous work and a wonder: for the wisdom of their wise men shall perish, and the understanding of their prudent men shall be hid.

CHERISHED GIFTS FROM GOD

Children are an heritage of the Lord.

CHOSEN ONES

Now therefore, if ye will obey my voice indeed, and keep my covenant, then ye shall be a peculiar treasure unto me above all people: for all the earth is mine: And ye shall be unto me a kingdom of priests, and an holy nation. These are the words which thou shalt speak unto the children of Israel.

CLAIM YOUR BLESSINGS! Application of Psalm 24:3–4

If we repent and live pure lives, then we are worthy to receive temple ordinances and enter the celestial kingdom.

CLEAN THROUGH HIM

Come now, and let us reason together, saith the Lord: though your sins be as scarlet, they shall be as white as snow; though they be red like crimson, they shall be as wool.

COMING PROMISE

Behold, now it is called today until the coming of the Son of Man, and verily it is a day of sacrifice, and a day for the tithing of my people; for he that is tithed shall not be burned at his coming.

COVENANT KEEPERS

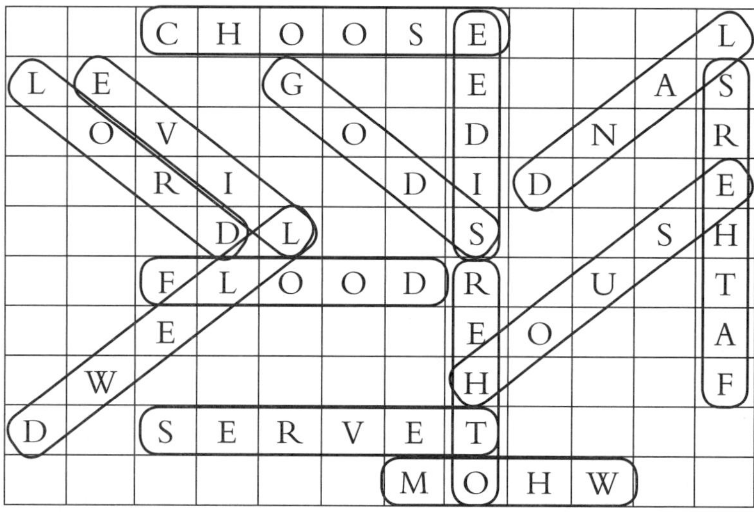

ESTABLISH MY WORDS

Wherefore, the Lord God will proceed to bring forth the words of the book; and in the mouth of as many witnesses as seemeth him good will he establish his word; and wo be unto him that rejecteth the word of God!

FEEL HIS PRESENCE NEAR

Answer: blessings

Is not this the fast that I have chosen? to loose the bands of wickedness, to undo the heavy burdens, and to let the oppressed go free, and that ye break every yoke? Is it not to deal thy bread to the hungry, and that thou bring the poor that are cast out to thy house? when thou seest the naked, that thou cover him; and that thou hide not thyself from thine own flesh?

FLEE TEMPTATION

There is none greater in this house than I; neither hath he kept back any thing from me but thee, because thou art his wife: how then can I do this great wickedness, and sin against God?

GUIDING BEACON

Thy word is a lamp unto my feet, and a light unto my path.

HONOR THIS DAY

If thou turn away thy foot from the sabbath, from doing thy pleasure on my holy day; and call the sabbath a delight, the holy of the Lord, honourable; and shalt honour him, not doing thine own ways, nor finding thine own pleasure, nor speaking thine own words: Then shalt thou delight thyself in the Lord; and I will cause thee to ride upon the high places of the earth, and feed thee with the heritage of Jacob thy father: for the mouth of the Lord hath spoken it.

I WILL, I WILL

Who shall ascend into the hill of the Lord? or who shall stand in his holy place?
He that hath clean hands, and a pure heart; who hath not lifted up his soul unto vanity, nor sworn deceitfully.

If we repent and live pure lives, then we are worthy to receive temple ordinances and enter the celestial kingdom.

LOOK INSIDE

But the Lord said unto Samuel, Look not on his countenance, or on the height of his stature; because I have refused him: for the Lord seeth not as man seeth; for man looketh on the outward appearance, but the Lord looketh on the heart.

MAN OF GRIEF

But he was wounded for our transgressions, he was bruised for our iniquities: the chastisement of our peace was upon him; and with his stripes we are healed.

MY GLORY

For behold, this is my work and my glory—to bring to pass the immortality and eternal life of man.

NEVER LED ASTRAY

Surely the Lord God will do nothing, but he revealeth his secret unto his servants the prophets.

NO MATTER WHAT

Key words: Trust in the Lord.

OFFERINGS AND BLESSINGS

Ye are cursed with a curse: for ye have robbed me, even this whole nation.

Bring ye all the tithes into the storehouse, that there may be meat in mine house, and prove me now herewith, saith the Lord of hosts, if I will not open you the windows of heaven, and pour you out a blessing, that there shall not be room enough to receive it.

ON THE SIXTH DAY

And God said, Let us make man in our image, after our likeness: and let them have dominion over the fish of the sea, and over the fowl of the air, and over the cattle, and over all the earth, and over every creeping thing that creepeth upon the earth. So God created man in his own image, in the image of God created he him; male and female created he them.

PRECIOUS ONES

Lo, children are an heritage of the Lord: and the fruit of the womb is his reward.

PREMORTAL BEINGS

Now the Lord had shown unto me, Abraham, the intelligences that were organized before the world was; and among all these there were many of the noble and great ones; And God saw these souls that they were good, and he stood in the midst of them, and he said: These I will make my rulers; for he stood among those that were spirits, and he saw that they were good; and he said unto me: Abraham, thou art one of them; thou wast chosen before thou wast born.

PRIESTHOOD KEYS RESTORED Malachi 4:5–6

Behold, I will send you Elijah the prophet before the coming of the great and dreadful day of the Lord: And he shall turn the heart of the fathers to the children, and the heart of the children to their fathers, lest I come and smite the earth with a curse.

PURIFIED BY OBEDIENCE Application of Exodus 19:5–6

Answer: Holy Nation

RELY ON HIS GUIDANCE

Trust in the Lord with all thine heart; and lean not unto thine own understanding. In all thy ways acknowledge him, and he shall direct thy paths.

THE LORD'S ERRAND Key words for Joshua 24:15

Choose to serve the Lord.

THE TEN COMMANDMENTS: PART 1

Answer: I am God Almighty

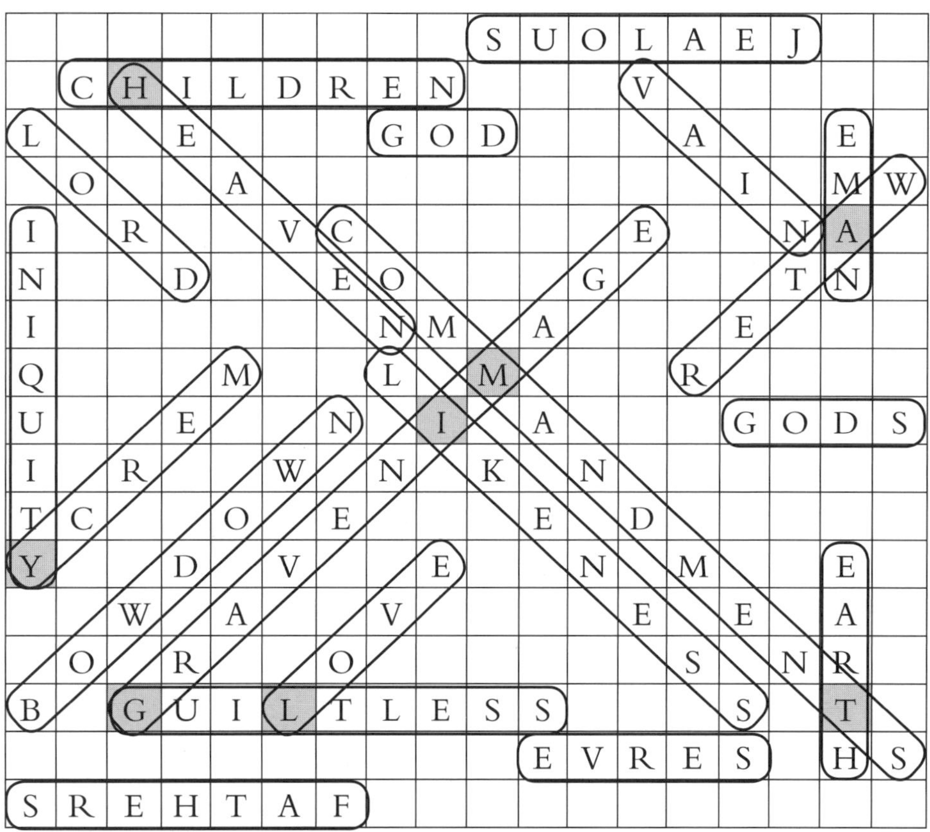

THE TEN COMMANDMENTS: PART 2

Answer: reverence

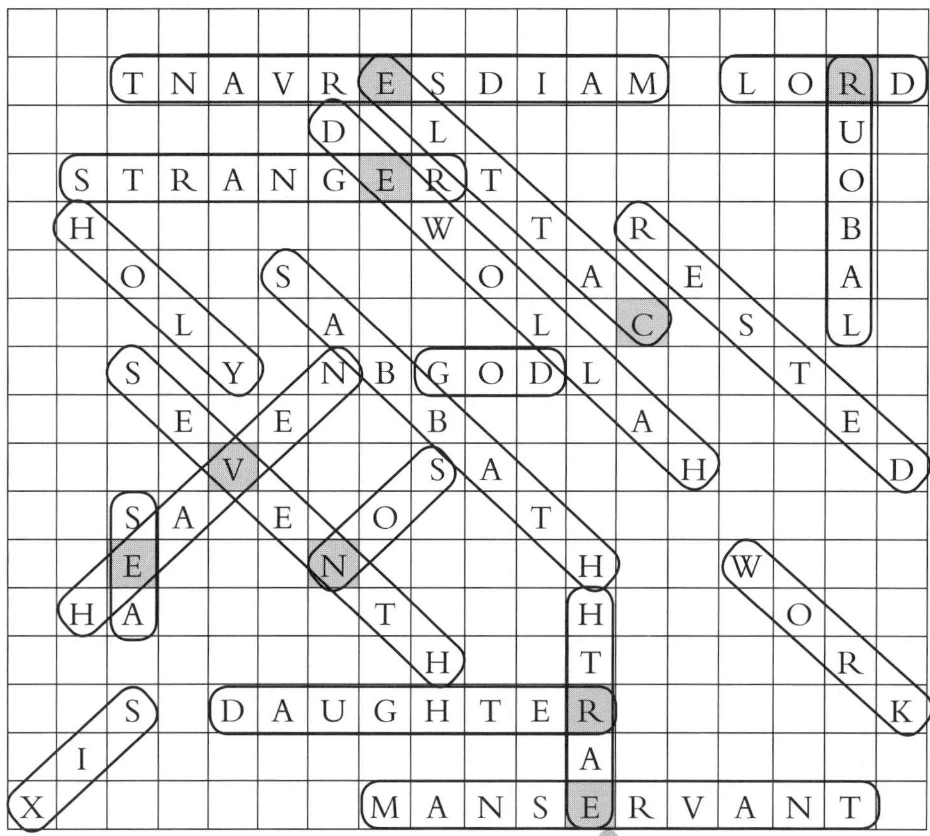

THE TEN COMMANDMENTS: PART 3 Answer: Divine guidance

TOGETHER FOREVER

Therefore shall a man leave his father and his mother, and shall cleave unto his wife: and they shall be one flesh.

Marriage between a man and a woman is <u>ordained</u> of God.

UNITED IN PURPOSE

And the Lord called his people Zion, because they were of one heart and one mind, and dwelt in righteousness; and there was no poor among them.

VOICE OF WARNING Application of Amos 3:7

God reveals His will through prophets.

WISE IN THEIR OWN EYES

Woe unto them that call evil good, and good evil; that put darkness for light, and light for darkness; that put bitter for sweet, and sweet for bitter!

WISE PURPOSE

Then the word of the Lord came unto me, saying, Before I formed thee in the belly I knew thee; and before thou camest forth out of the womb I sanctified thee, and I ordained thee a prophet unto the nations.

NEW TESTAMENT

ANSWER KEY

A CITY SET ON A HILL

Let your light so shine.

A HOUSE OF GOD

What? know ye not that your body is the temple of the Holy Ghost which is in you, which ye have of God, and ye are not your own? For ye are bought with a price: therefore glorify God in your body, and in your spirit, which are God's.

A SACRED GIFT

Answer: Your body is holy.

										C					M
	W							H	T	L	A	E	H		S
		O	R			C		C		E					I
	I		R	E			H			A					T
	M			D	S	O		A		N					P
	A				O	P			S						A
	G			S	L	F	E			T	H	T	R	I	B
	E		E		A		W	C			I				
	O			T	C			I	T			T			
	F				I				S	H	O	L	Y		D
	G				S	R		M	O	D	E	S	T	Y	E
W	O	R	T	H	Y		I				O				R
	D				H			P				M			C
					P				S						A
					T	E	M	P	T	A	T	I	O	N	S

ALL WILL LIVE AGAIN

In Christ shall all be resurrected.

ALWAYS NEAR

Jesus can strengthen us to do whatever God requires of us.

ASCENSION FOR ALL

But now is Christ risen from the dead, and become the firstfruits of them that slept. For since by man came death, by man came also the resurrection of the dead. For as in Adam all die, even so in Christ shall all be made alive.

ASK TO KNOW

God willingly gives wisdom to those who ask of Him in faith.

BE BAPTIZED

Jesus answered, Verily, verily, I say unto thee, Except a man be born of water and of the Spirit, he cannot enter into the kingdom of God.

BE NOT AFRAID

And as they thus spake, Jesus himself stood in the midst of them, and saith unto them, Peace be unto you. But they were terrified and affrighted, and supposed that they had seen a spirit. And he said unto them, Why are ye troubled? and why do thoughts arise in your hearts? Behold my hands and my feet, that it is I myself: handle me, and see; for a spirit hath not flesh and bones, as ye see me have.

BOUNTEOUS BLESSINGS

But the fruit of the Spirit is love, joy, peace, longsuffering, gentleness, goodness, faith, meekness, temperance: against such there is no law.

DIVINE GUIDANCE

If any of you lack wisdom, let him ask of God, that giveth to all men liberally, and upbraideth not; and it shall be given him. But let him ask in faith, nothing wavering. For he that wavereth is like a wave of the sea driven with the wind and tossed.

EVERLASTING BLESSING

And this is life eternal, that they might know thee the only true God, and Jesus Christ, whom thou hast sent.

Testimony

FIND REFUGE IN ME

Come unto me, all ye that labour and are heavy laden, and I will give you rest.
Take my yoke upon you, and learn of me; for I am meek and lowly in heart: and ye shall find rest unto your souls. For my yoke is easy, and my burden is light.

If we come unto Jesus Christ, He will ease our burdens.

FOREVER BOUND

He saith unto them, But whom say ye that I am? And Simon Peter answered and said, Thou art the Christ, the Son of the living God. And Jesus answered and said unto him, Blessed art thou, Simon Bar-jona: for flesh and blood hath not revealed it unto thee, but my Father which is in heaven. And I say also unto thee, That thou art Peter, and upon this rock I will build my church; and the gates of hell shall not prevail against it. And I will give unto thee the keys of the kingdom of heaven: and whatsoever thou shalt bind on earth shall be bound in heaven: and whatsoever thou shalt loose on earth shall be loosed in heaven.

GOOD NEWS FOR ALL

For for this cause was the gospel preached also to them that are dead, that they might be judged according to men in the flesh, but live according to God in the spirit.

HEAVENLY KINGDOMS

There are also celestial bodies, and bodies terrestrial: but the glory of the celestial is one, and the glory of the terrestrial is another. There is one glory of the sun, and another glory of the moon, and another glory of the stars: for one star differeth from another star in glory. So also is the resurrection of the dead. It is sown in corruption; it is raised in incorruption.

HELP FROM ON HIGH

I can do all things through Christ which strengtheneth me.

HOW CAN WE KNOW THE WAY?

Jesus saith unto him, I am the way, the truth, and the life: no man cometh unto the Father, but by me.

JUDGMENT DAY

And I saw the dead, small and great, stand before God; and the books were opened: and another book was opened, which is the book of life: and the dead were judged out of those things which were written in the books, according to their works.

PERFECTED STATE

Jesus Christ is a resurrected being. A resurrected body is a body of flesh and bones.

PREPARE FOR BLESSINGS

Repentance and baptism for the remission of sins prepare us to receive the gift of Holy Ghost.

RESTITUTION FORETOLD

Repent ye therefore, and be converted, that your sins may be blotted out, when the times of refreshing shall come from the presence of the Lord; And he shall send Jesus Christ, which before was preached unto you: Whom the heaven must receive until the times of restitution of all things, which God hath spoken by the mouth of all his holy prophets since the world began.

Prophecies

SHINE ON!

Ye are the light of the world. A city that is set on an hill cannot be hid.

Neither do men light a candle, and put it under a bushel, but on a candlestick; and it giveth light unto all that are in the house. Let your light so shine before men, that they may see your good works, and glorify your Father which is in heaven.

TEACH AND BAPTIZE

Go ye therefore, and teach all nations, baptizing them in the name of the Father, and of the Son, and of the Holy Ghost: teaching them to observe all things whatsoever I have commanded you: and, lo, I am with you alway, even unto the end of the world. Amen.

THE GOOD FIGHT

Even so faith, if it hath not works, is dead, being alone. Yea, a man may say, Thou hast faith, and I have works: shew me thy faith without thy works, and I will shew thee my faith by my works.

THE GREATEST TWO

Master, which is the great commandment in the law? Jesus said unto him, Thou shalt love the Lord thy God with all thy heart, and with all thy soul, and with all thy mind. This is the first and great commandment. And the second is like unto it, Thou shalt love thy neighbour as thyself.

THE REASON WE OBEY

If ye love me, keep my commandments.

1. serve
2. prayer
3. immersion
4. kingdoms
5. immortality
6. perfect

THEIR TEACHINGS

Abraham—obedience
Adam—plan of salvation
Daniel—law of health
Elijah—sealing power
Isaiah—prophesied of Savior
Jacob—faithful patriarch
Jonah—missionary work
Malachi—tithing
Moses—commandments
Noah—prepare
Samuel—seer and revelator

TO PERFECT US

And he gave some, apostles; and some, prophets; and some, evangelists; and some, pastors and teachers; for the perfecting of the saints, for the work of the ministry, for the edifying of the body of Christ.

WALK IN THE SPIRIT

Kingdom of God

WHAT SHALL WE DO? Theme: Follow Him

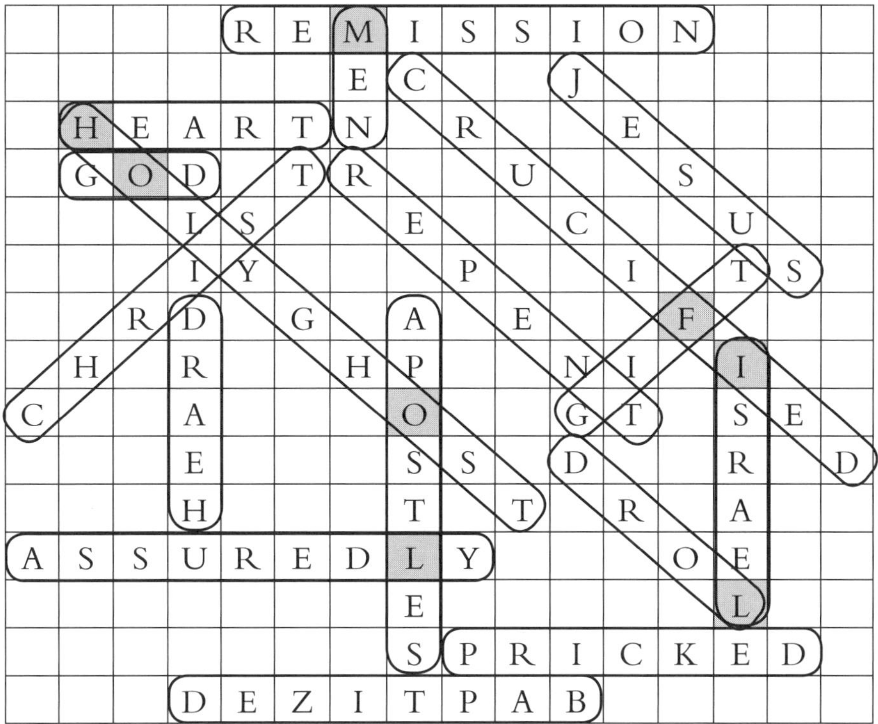

WHEN WILL HE COME?

Now we beseech you, brethren, by the coming of our Lord Jesus Christ, and by our gathering together unto him, That ye be not soon shaken in mind, or be troubled, neither by spirit, nor by word, nor by letter as from us, as that the day of Christ is at hand. Let no man deceive you by any means: for that day shall not come, except there come a falling away first, and that man of sin be revealed, the son of perdition.

WHOM THE LORD LOVES

Furthermore we have had fathers of our flesh which corrected us, and we gave them reverence: shall we not much rather be in subjection unto the Father of spirits, and live?

WITH ALL THY HEART

Yea, come unto Christ, and be perfected in him, and deny yourselves of all ungodliness; and if ye shall deny yourselves of all ungodliness, and love God with all your might, mind and strength, then is his grace sufficient for you, that by his grace ye may be perfect in Christ; and if by the grace of God ye are perfect in Christ, ye can in nowise deny the power of God. (Moroni 10:32)

WORDS OF INSPIRATION

And that from a child thou hast known the holy scriptures, which are able to make thee wise unto salvation through faith which is in Christ Jesus. All scripture is given by inspiration of God, and is profitable for doctrine, for reproof, for correction, for instruction in righteousness: That the man of God may be perfect, throughly furnished unto all good works.

BOOK OF MORMON

ANSWER KEY

A PARTICLE

And now as I said concerning faith—faith is not to have a perfect knowledge of things; therefore if ye have faith ye hope for things which are not seen, which are true.

AGENCY

Wherefore, men are free according to the flesh; and all things are given them which are expedient unto man. And they are free to choose liberty and eternal life, through the great Mediator of all men, or to choose captivity and death, according to the captivity and power of the devil; for he seeketh that all men might be miserable like unto himself.

BE OBEDIENT

And it came to pass that I, Nephi, said unto my father: I will go and do the things which the Lord hath commanded, for I know that the Lord giveth no commandments unto the children of men, save he shall prepare a way for them that they may accomplish the thing which he commandeth them.

BE TEACHABLE

										N	A	T	U	R	A	L	M	A	N					
	E	N	E	M	Y	T	O	G	O	D														
								F	A	L	L	O	F	A	D	A	M							
						F	O	R	E	V	E	R												
	E	N	T	I	C	I	N	G	S	O	F	T	H	E	H	O	L	Y	S	P	I	R	I	T
B	E	C	O	M	E	T	H	A	S	A	I	N	T											
	A	T	O	N	E	M	E	N	T	O	F	C	H	R	I	S	T	T	H	E	L	O	R	D
									B	E	C	O	M	E	T	H	A	S	A	C	H	I	L	D
		S	U	B	M	I	S	S	I	V	E										M	E	E	K
												H	U	M	B	L	E							
	P	A	T	I	E	N	T		F	U	L	L	O	F	L	O	V	E						
							W	I	L	L	I	N	G	T	O	S	U	B	M	I	T			

BE WISE

And behold, I tell you these things that ye may learn wisdom; that ye may learn that when ye are in the service of your fellow beings ye are only in the service of your God.

BECOMING STRONG

And if men come unto me I will show unto them their weakness. I give unto men weakness that they may be humble; and my grace is sufficient for all men that humble themselves before me; for if they humble themselves before me, and have faith in me, then will I make weak things become strong unto them.

BLESSINGS ARE YOURS

And what is it that ye shall hope for? Behold I say unto you that ye shall have hope through the atonement of Christ and the power of his resurrection, to be raised unto life eternal, and this because of your faith in him according to the promise.

BUILD ON THE ROCK

And now, my sons, remember, remember that it is upon the rock of our Redeemer, who is Christ, the Son of God, that ye must build your foundation; that when the devil shall send forth his mighty winds, yea, his shafts in the whirlwind, yea, when all his hail and his mighty storm shall beat upon you, it shall have no power over you to drag you down to the gulf of misery and endless wo, because of the rock upon which ye are built, which is a sure foundation, a foundation whereon if men build they cannot fall.

CENTERED ON THE SAVIOR

Have hope through the Atonement of Christ.

CHILDREN, BE WISE

Learn in thy youth to keep the commandments.

CHOOSE THE RIGHT

O, remember, my son, and learn wisdom in thy youth; yea, learn in thy youth to keep the commandments of God.

DOUBT NOT, FEAR NOT

Across

2. Holy Ghost
4. Jesus Christ
7. unshaken
9. humble
10. diligence
11. witness
12. believe

Down

1. prayers
2. hope
3. trust
5. righteousness
6. knowledge
8. patience

HE WILL BLESS YOU

And now, my beloved brethren, I perceive that ye ponder still in your hearts; and it grieveth me that I must speak concerning this thing. For if ye would hearken unto the Spirit which teacheth a man to pray, ye would know that ye must pray; for the evil spirit teacheth not a man to pray, but teacheth him that he must not pray. But behold, I say unto you that ye must pray always, and not faint; that ye must not perform any thing unto the Lord save in the first place ye shall pray unto the Father in the name of Christ, that he will consecrate thy performance unto thee, that thy performance may be for the welfare of thy soul.

HIS TRANSGRESSION

Adam fell that men might be; and men are, that they might have joy.

LIKE OUR FATHER

Therefore I would that ye should be perfect even as I, or your Father who is in heaven is perfect.

LINE UPON LINE

Learn in they youth to keep the commandments.

Helaman

LULL THEM AWAY

In the last days, many will teach false, vain, and foolish doctrines.

OBEDIENCE BRINGS JOY

Do not suppose, because it has been spoken concerning restoration, that ye shall be restored from sin to happiness. Behold, I say unto you, wickedness never was happiness.

PLAIN WORDS

Feast on the words of Christ.

PRESS FORWARD

And now, my beloved brethren, after ye have gotten into this strait and narrow path, I would ask if all is done? Behold, I say unto you, Nay; for ye have not come thus far save it were by the word of Christ with unshaken faith in him, relying wholly upon the merits of him who is mighty to save. Wherefore, ye must press forward with a steadfastness in Christ, having a perfect brightness of hope, and a love of God and of all men. Wherefore, if ye shall press forward, feasting upon the word of Christ, and endure to the end, behold, thus saith the Father: Ye shall have eternal life.

SINCERE PRAYER

And when ye shall receive these things, I would exhort you that ye would ask God, the Eternal Father, in the name of Christ, if these things are not true; and if ye shall ask with a sincere heart, with real intent, having faith in Christ, he will manifest the truth of it unto you, by the power of the Holy Ghost. And by the power of the Holy Ghost ye may know the truth of all things.

SURE FOUNDATION

Only by basing our lives on Jesus Christ can we withstand Satan's temptations.

THE COMFORTER TESTIFIES

The Holy Ghost reveals truth.

THE GREATEST OF ALL

Charity

	S	O	N	S		P	O	S	S	E	S	S	E	D
S	F	H	T	E	I	V	N	E					D	
	U	O	B	E	L	E	I	V	E	T	H	N		
		F	R			I	N	I	Q	U	I	T	Y	
			F	E						K		G		
				E	V		W	E	L	L	R		E	D
H	E	A	R	T	R	E				E		P	E	
S	F		P			E	R	H	N		O	I	E	H
E		I		P		B	T	E		H	F	T	V	T
E	H		L		E	U	E	H		I	S	P	O	E
K	O	S		L	R	A		A	R	I		R	L	R
E	P		E	T	E		R	U	R			A	E	U
T	E			E		D	P	H		E		Y	R	D
H	T	R	E	J	O	I	C	E	T	H	T		U	N
T	H	I	N	K	E	T	H					H	P	E

THE LORD'S HANDS

give and help

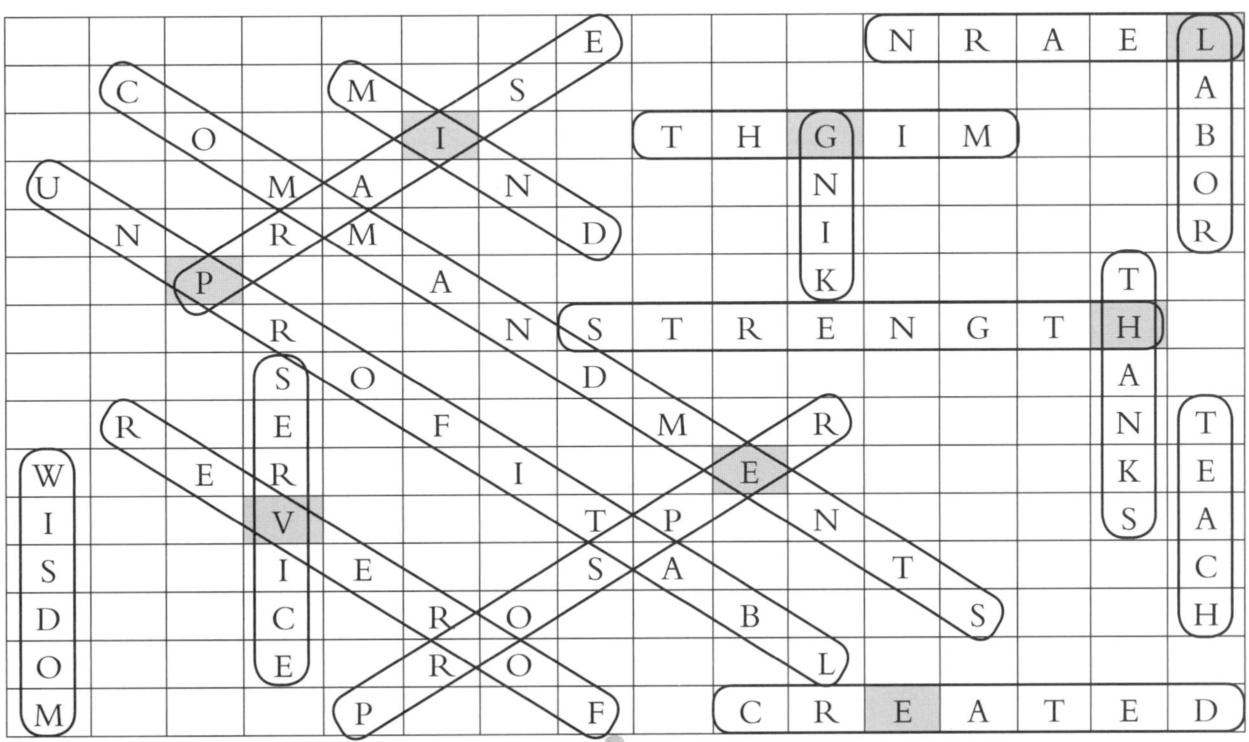

THE PRECEPTS OF MEN

Yea, and there shall be many which shall say: Eat, drink, and be merry, for tomorrow we die; and it shall be well with us. And there shall also be many which shall say: Eat, drink, and be merry; nevertheless, fear God—he will justify in committing a little sin; yea, lie a little, take the advantage of one because of his words, dig a pit for thy neighbor; there is no harm in this; and do all these things, for tomorrow we die; and if it so be that we are guilty, God will beat us with a few stripes, and at last we shall be saved in the kingdom of God. Yea, and there shall be many which shall teach after this manner, false and vain and foolish doctrines, and shall be puffed up in their hearts, and shall seek deep to hide their counsels from the Lord; and their works shall be in the dark.

THESE THINGS WE DO

	B	E	L	I	E	V	E				
P							T				T
R				E			I			A	
E	E				C		R		L		
A		C				I	W	K			P
C			O				O				E
H	R			N				J			R
	O			K	C				E		S
	B		O			I				R	U
	A	O					L				A
	L		P	R	O	P	H	E	S	Y	D
									D		E
			E	C	A	R	G				

THEY SPEAK FOR HIM

Angels speak by the power of the Holy Ghost; wherefore, they speak the words of Christ. Wherefore, I said unto you, feast upon the words of Christ; for behold, the words of Christ will tell you all things what ye should do.

TO SAVE OUR SOULS

And he shall go forth, suffering pains and afflictions and temptations of every kind; and this that the word might be fulfilled which saith he will take upon him the pains and the sicknesses of his people. And he will take upon him death, that he may loose the bands of death which bind his people; and he will take upon him their infirmities, that his bowels may be filled with mercy, according to the flesh, that he may know according to the flesh how to succor his people according to their infirmities. Now the Spirit knoweth all things; nevertheless the Son of God suffereth according to the flesh that he might take upon him the sins of his people, that he might blot out their transgressions according to the power of his deliverance; and now behold, this is the testimony which is in me.

TO THE END

But this much I can tell you, that if ye do not watch yourselves, and your thoughts, and your words, and your deeds, and observe the commandments of God, and continue in the faith of what ye have heard concerning the coming of our Lord, even unto the end of your lives, ye must perish. And now, O man, remember, and perish not.

TRUE WISDOM

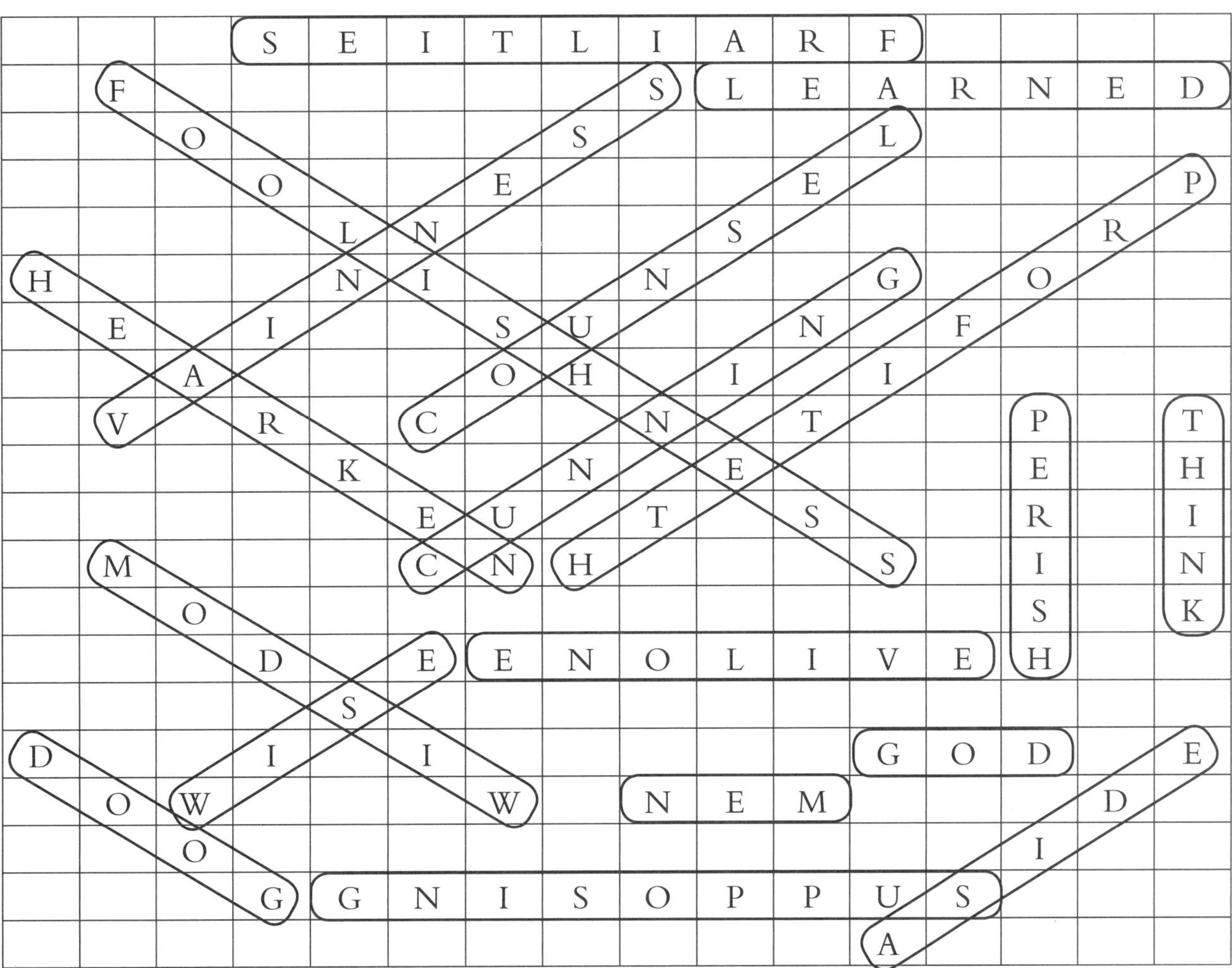

TURN FROM IT

Now my son, I would that ye should repent and forsake your sins, and go no more after the lusts of your eyes, but cross yourself in all these things; for except ye do this ye can in nowise inherit the kingdom of God. Oh, remember, and take it upon you, and cross yourself in these things.

UNSEEN TRUTH

And now, I, Moroni, would speak somewhat concerning these things; I would show unto the world that faith is things which are hoped for and not seen; wherefore, dispute not because ye see not, for ye receive no witness until after the trial of your faith.

WATCH AND PRAY ALWAYS

Verily, verily, I say unto you, ye must watch and pray always, lest ye be tempted by the devil, and ye be led away captive by him.

And whatsoever ye shall ask the Father in my name, which is right, believing that ye shall receive, behold it shall be given unto you.

Pray in your families unto the Father, always in my name, that your wives and your children may be blessed.

WE DO BELIEVE

For we labor diligently to write, to persuade our children, and also our brethren, to believe in Christ, and to be reconciled to God; for we know that it is by grace that we are saved, after all we can do.

And we talk of Christ, we rejoice in Christ, we preach of Christ, we prophesy of Christ, and we write according to our prophecies, that our children may know to what source they may look for a remission of their sins.

YIELD TO THE HOLY GHOST

natural man

1. patient
2. Fall of Adam
3. enticings
4. submit
5. Christ
6. Atonement
7. humble
8. meek
9. Saints
10. enemy

DOCTRINE AND COVENANTS

ANSWER KEY

A PRINCIPLE WITH PROMISE

obedience

o. wheat for man
b. strong drinks (are not for the belly)
e. flesh . . . of beasts and . . . fowls
d. hot drinks (are not for the body)
i. all wholesome herbs
e. adapted to the capacity of the weak
n. all grain
c. fruit of the vine
e. tobacco (is not for the body)

A PROMISE

I, the Lord, am bound when ye do what I say; but when ye do not what I say, ye have no promise.

ALL SAINTS

And all saints who remember to keep and do these sayings, walking in obedience to the commandments, shall receive health in their navel and marrow to their bones; And shall find wisdom and great treasures of knowledge, even hidden treasures; And shall run and not be weary, and shall walk and not faint. And I, the Lord, give unto them a promise, that the destroying angel shall pass by them, as the children of Israel, and not slay them. Amen.

APPEARANCES

The First Vision

CELESTIAL GLORY

And in order to obtain the highest, a man must enter into this order of the priesthood [meaning the new and everlasting covenant of marriage].

COME FOLLOW ME

Learn of me, and listen to my words; walk in the meekness of my Spirit, and you shall have peace in me.

DO GOOD

Verily I say, men should be anxiously engaged in a good cause, and do many things of their own free will, and bring to pass much righteousness.

FINDING JOY IN STRENGTH

Cease to be idle; cease to be unclean; cease to find fault one with another; cease to sleep longer than is needful; retire to thy bed early, that ye may not be weary; arise early, that your bodies and your minds may be invigorated.

FOR ALL

For behold, I, God, have suffered these things for all, that they might not suffer if they would repent; But if they would not repent they must suffer even as I;

Which suffering caused myself, even God, the greatest of all, to tremble because of pain, and to bleed at every pore, and to suffer both body and spirit—and would that I might not drink the bitter cup, and shrink.

FORGIVE ONE ANOTHER

And ye ought to say in your hearts—let God judge between me and thee, and reward thee according to thy deeds.

FULL HEART

Across	Down
2. praise	1. honor
5. gratitude	3. rejoice
7. increase	4. blessing
8. grateful	6. thankful

GIFTS OF THE SPIRIT

And ye must practice virtue and holiness before me continually. Even so. Amen.

GRATEFUL HEART

And he who receiveth all things with thankfulness shall be made glorious; and the things of this earth shall be added unto him, even an hundred fold, yea, more.

Receive all things with thankfulness.

HE CAME

And this is the gospel, the glad tidings, which the voice out of the heavens bore record unto us—That he came into the world, even Jesus, to be crucified for the world, and to bear the sins of the world, and to sanctify the world, and to cleanse it from all unrighteousness.

HEAR MY VOICE

Yea, behold, I will tell you in your mind and in your heart, by the Holy Ghost, which shall come upon you and which shall dwell in your heart.

Now, behold, this is the spirit of revelation; behold, this is the spirit by which Moses brought the children of Israel through the Red Sea on dry ground.

HEAVENLY COMMUNICATION

											M								
	S						E		R		A								
M		T				R		E			N								S
A			I		A		V				I							N	
K				L		E		G			F						G		
E			C		L			U			E		I	E	N	I	V	I	D
K		E		A		S		I			S		N		S				
N	D		T				M	D			T		S						
O		I		L				A					P						
W	O			A		M		N	L				I						
N				E		I		C		L			R		S	H	O	W	
	D			V		A		E			V		A						
	R			E		L				Y		O	T						
	E			R		C			C				I						
	A					O		E					O	C					N
	M					R	H						N		E			O	
						P											I		
					O		D	I	S	C	L	O	S	E		S			
				R											I				
			P		T	S	O	H	G	Y	L	O	H	V					

HIGHER POWER

The Melchizedek Priesthood holds the right of presidency, and has power and authority over all the offices in the church in all ages of the world, to administer in spiritual things.

The Melchizedek is the greater priesthood.

IN HIS IMAGE

The Father has a body of flesh and bones as tangible as man's; the Son also; but the Holy Ghost has not a body of flesh and bones, but is a personage of Spirit. Were it not so, the Holy Ghost could not dwell in us. A man may receive the Holy Ghost, and it may descend upon him and not tarry with him.

IN THE LIGHT

	N	A													
P	O		D				D	E	L	E	E	N	K		D
	I			V							O			E	P
	T	L			E					S			L		E
	I		L			R			D			I			R
	S			A			S	E			V				S
	O				R		V	A		E				M	O
	P					O			R				E		N
G	P	J			L		F			Y		H			A
	O		O	E				L			T				G
		D	B	I				R	I	F				S	E
					N		E		O	G				E	S
	R					W		E			H			N	
		I			O		N					T		I	
		N	G	P	G	O	D	L	I	N	E	S	S	R	
		Q		H	N									T	
		U			T									C	
	D	I	S	T	U	R	B	E	R					O	
		R					S	S	E	N	K	R	A	D	
		E		S	T	R	A	E	H						

JESUS CHRIST LIVES

D	R	O	C	E	R	G	N	I	R	A	E	B			
			T											R	
		S	E	V	I	L	E	H	T	A	H	T		I	
	V		S							N			S	G	
		O	T							E			T	H	
			I						L	T			N	T	
			M	C				L		T			A	H	
			O		E		A	T		O			T	A	
			N			F	H			G			I	N	
			I		O	R				E			B	D	
			E	T	O					B			A		
			S	U						Y			H		
		A	G							L		M	N		
	L	H								N			I		
			S	D	L	R	O	W		O				H	
S	O	N	S	A	N	D	D	A	U	G	H	T	E	R	S

JOY AND COMFORT

Wherefore, lift up thy heart and rejoice, and cleave unto the covenants which thou hast made.

KEYS TO BAPTIZE

The Aaronic Priesthood was restored.

LISTEN

Learn of the Savior and listen to His words.

OBEY THE LAW

And when we obtain any blessing from God, it is by obedience to that law upon which it is predicated.

OUR LIKENESS

The Father and Son have bodies of flesh and bones.

POWER AND INFLUENCE

Across	Down
1. guile	1. gentleness
3. without	2. love
7. pure	4. hypocrisy
9. priesthood	5. persuasion
11. meekness	6. knowledge
13. long-suffering	8. enlarge
14. kindness	10. unfeigned
	12. soul

POWER TO BLESS

The Melchizedek Priesthood is the greater priesthood and administers in spiritual things.

POWERFUL PRINCIPLES

That the rights of the priesthood are inseparably connected with the powers of heaven, and that the powers of heaven cannot be controlled nor handled only upon the principles of righteousness.

PREACH UNTO THE WORLD

Across	Down
2. mission	1. Christ
4. repentance	3. service
6. faith	5. commandments
10. Lord	6. foundation
11. Son	7. Holy Ghost
12. teach	8. worship
13. gospel	9. baptize
14. Jesus	11. souls

PRIESTHOOD POWER

Upon you my fellow servants, in the name of Messiah I confer the Priesthood of Aaron, which holds the keys of the ministering of angels, and of the gospel of repentance, and of baptism by immersion for the remission of sins; and this shall never be taken again from the earth, until the sons of Levi do offer again an offering unto the Lord in righteousness.

The Priesthood of Aaron is the authority to baptize.

SAVE OUR WORLD FROM SIN

The Redeemer

									S	O	N	O	F	G	O	D	
						T	E	S	T	I	M	O	N	Y	O		
Y		D	R	I	H	T		T						O			D
F									E				L				E
I			D	E	I	F	I	C	U	R	C	B					T
T						D				Y	N						C
C					E	T			R			A					E
N				V			N	A	R				L			V	R
A			A				V	E		B				L	I		R
S		S				L	H		M					G	I		U
	P				A	T		A		E			R			F	S
	O			C	A		L				N	O					E
	W			F							F	O					R
	E												T				
C	R	O	S	S										A			

SEARCH THE SCRIPTURES

Search these commandments, for they are true and faithful, and the prophecies and promises which are in them shall all be fulfilled.

What I the Lord have spoken, I have spoken, and I excuse not myself; and though the heavens and the earth pass away, my word shall not pass away, but shall all be fulfilled, whether by mine own voice or by the voice of my servants, it is the same.

THE BITTER CUP

Nevertheless, glory be to the Father, and I partook and finished my preparations unto the children of men.

THY WILL BE DONE

Jesus Christ's words shall all be fulfilled.

TO OVERCOME

Pray always, that you may come off conqueror; yea, that you may conquer Satan, and that you may escape the hands of the servants of Satan that do uphold his work.

WHAT'S IT WORTH?

Remember the worth of souls is great in the sight of God; for, behold, the Lord your Redeemer suffered death in the flesh; wherefore he suffered the pain of all men, that all men might repent and come unto him.

WHERE DO I LOOK?

Look unto Christ.

WITHOUT FEAR

Look unto me in every thought; doubt not, fear not.

WORK TO SAVE SOULS

And if it so be that you should labor all your days in crying repentance unto this people, and bring, save it be one soul unto me, how great shall be your joy with him in the kingdom of my Father! And now, if your joy will be great with one soul that you have brought unto me into the kingdom of my Father, how great will be your joy if you should bring many souls unto me!

YOU ARE FORGIVEN

Behold, he who has repented of his sins, the same is forgiven, and I, the Lord, remember them no more. By this ye may know if a man repenteth of his sins—behold, he will confess them and forsake them.

ABOUT MARYALICE

MaryAlice Wallis is the coauthor of the award winning *LDS Puzzle Pals* and *LDS Puzzle Pals: Prophets and Apostles*. She graduated from Western Washington University with a degree in speech pathology and audiology. She is an original member of the Golden Quill Writers Group in Southwest Washington. She is currently writing a homeschooling resource book. MaryAlice and her husband, David, homeschooled their four children and are experiencing life as half-empty nesters. Their family loves traveling to the beach from their home in the Pacific Northwest. Sunshine, sand, and a good book will keep her occupied for hours. MaryAlice currently serves as the stake Relief Society president.

ABOUT CHARLOTTE

Charlotte Lindstrom is the coauthor of two other puzzle books: *LDS Puzzle Pals* and *LDS Puzzle Pals: Prophets and Apostles*. She has written many puzzles for the *Friend* magazine and has stories published in the *Friend*, the *New Era*, and *Cricket* magazines. She is an original member of the Golden Quill Writers Group in southwest Washington. She is also a member of the American Night Writers Association (ANWA). A graduate of Utah State University, she currently teaches second grade in Longview, Washington. Charlotte is a puzzler, reader, family history buff, quilter, and writer. She lives in Longview, Washington, with her husband, Dan. She currently serves as the stake public affairs director with her husband.